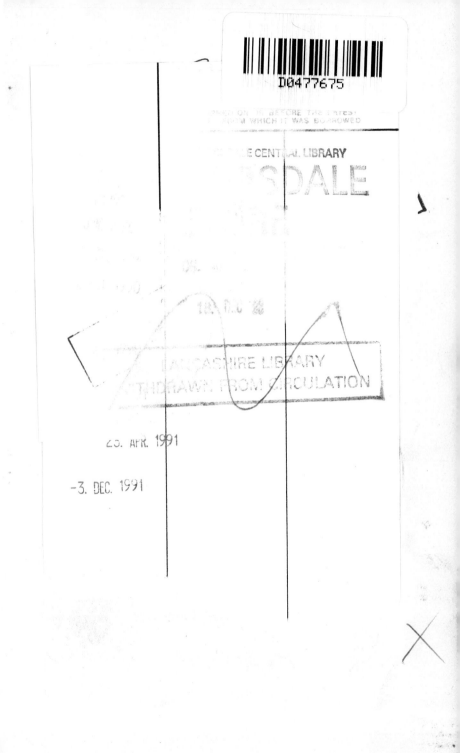

Mathilde Carré:
Double Agent

Mathilde Carré: Double Agent

LAURAN PAINE

ROBERT HALE & COMPANY

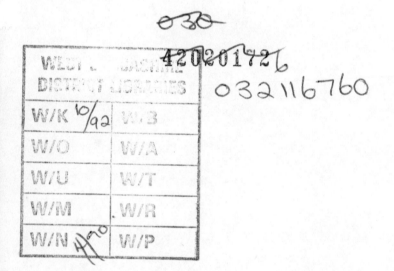

Contents

Illustrations

All photographs by permission of Keystone Press

Preface

Mathilde Carré was born in the closing year of the first decade
of the twentieth century when most people still believed in the
leisurely approach to all things, including crises. She matured
in the twilight before the long night of the Second World War,
and like millions of other human beings she was not in the
least prepared for the unbelievably swift holocaust unleashed
upon the world by Nazi Germany beginning in 1939. With the
fall of France, Mathilde's complex character accepted the
inevitable with the firm resolve that she would survive,
regardless of the cost.

This biography of Mathilde Carré details her intrigues, her
schemes, and her treacheries, all based upon that one
compulsion: survival. It helped immeasurably that Mathilde
was also vain, callous, self-centred and over-sexed. She was
capable of remorseless hypocrisy and convincing dramatics.
She was the least desirable woman for desperate men to know
and be compelled to rely upon, but in those desperate days
many men did rely on her, and some paid for that reliance and
trust with their lives.

Lauran Paine

1
Different Worlds

The tempo of historic epochs could be as leisurely as a Viennese waltz. Prior to the advent of the twentieth century, when communications were uncertain, when transportation was still only in part divorced from the horse, and when events which affected the lives of many people transpired, without fanfare or even immediate repercussions, it was generally accepted that history's great moments were a long time arriving, and a long time departing. The normal tenure of human existence was leisurely. History was not made in hours or days, or even months.

There had been some innovations; steam had to a respectable extent replaced sail. But it was still a high wind from astern that could drive the clippers ahead of the ironclads, and it was still a British Lion astride the sea-lanes, and manning the outposts of empire, that compelled a *status quo*. James Wolfe's ascent of the Heights of Abraham, his stunning defeat of Louis-Joseph de Montcalm in 1759, upset a balance, to be certain: France lost Canada, but the triumph was long in coming and predictable, and it altered men's lives very little, for a full generation.

Between the years, 1759 and 1859, a full century, although Britain's first empire crumbled and her second empire rose grander than the first, it required all that time to compel these events. Nations neither died nor were born in less time. Momentous conflicts were months in the planning stages, months in their repercussions, and years in their echoing resonance.

In the final decade of the nineteenth century, an appropriate ceremony signalled the end of these centuries-long and leisurely epochs: Britain's Diamond Jubilee, celebrating Queen Victoria's fifty-year reign.

As an event it was a long time in the planning, and was an even longer time in passing. It commemorated three enduring, grand achievements: Victoria's momentous years as Monarch, the high tide of Britain's empire, and the *Pax Brittanica*, a period when no great wars erupted, although innumerable small ones did.

Throughout several leisurely decades there existed a time of unprecedented peace, forced upon a contentious world by the master-players of London. Global diplomacy, sustained by the world's greatest war fleet, could, and did, blockade the ports and compel the homage of larger nations with greater armies, who required free access to the high seas to attempt conquests – which they dared not attempt without British sanction – and that was not forthcoming. Britain, master of the deep water, enforced peace – and ruled the largest ever English-speaking empire.

A Colonial Secretary, Joseph Chamberlain, said: "England without an empire! Can you conceive it?" No one could, not after all those decades of slow, careful growth, of leisurely devising and sustaining.

But Queen Victoria's year, 1897, great and historic as it undeniably was, the culmination of all those decades and generations of unhurried conquest and accomplishment, was also the last song of trimph, the final paean for a world of predictable and orderly sequences. Three years later the old century ended. Victoria survived her jubilee year by four years, dying in 1901, when an entire fresh set of stresses was tending towards totally altered conditions, under unpredictable circumstances. The last sail came down, the next-to-last horse caisson yielded to horseless power; men dared the sea from the underside, and the entire tempo of life gained momentum. People spoke of aerial flight, then accomplished it. Between the Diamond Jubilee, and the decade following Victoria's passing, the power that governed the sea lost its grip on the land. Hegemony atrophied when pan-Germanism could triumph without having to go to sea. The day of leisurely sequences had passed. No one fully realized how thoroughly it had passed, and the awakening to reality stunned even those who were the first to abandon tradition, the first to attempt blitz-conquest.

In 1914, the last vestiges of an old order were irretrievably shattered. France's traditionalism dissolved before Germany's onslaught, and what had theretofore been unthinkable, occurred. Pan-Germanism failed, which had been almost inevitable, but in the aftermath, in the long hush of late 1918, in that silent winter of retrospect and assessment, that which had happened, and which had not been possible before, was clear. In France, one million of the French lay dead. A quarter of a million buildings had been destroyed, 700,000 acres of land had been rendered uncultivatable. In Belgium, the lowlands, even in Germany, the comparable ruin was appalling. Within four years a loss in human lives in excess of Britain's total population the year George III became monarch, over eight and a half million people, perished as a result of warfare. It had not been possible before to accomplish such a carnage in so short a length of time.

The last casualty was an environment. The one celebrated so resoundingly in 1897. From 1914 onward the tempo of human existence achieved a momentum, and created an expanding vortex, which became indifferent to the efforts of thoughtful men to control it. It now was possible to obliterate entire nations, and with the loss of control went other vestiges of those earlier, leisurely epochs, such as dignity, feeling, a powerful spirituality, and human honour. Treason, which had once been recognised as the most inexcusable crime, having succeeded in 1914, having flourished subsequently, was encouraged and cultivated.

It was not novel to history, but since the dominant vitality of the European non-Latins held treason and treachery to be a paramount crime, and the minds of these people did not revel in Italianate subtleties, an individual who pratised the political heresy of espionage, for example, was rewarded with death, if apprehended. Nevertheless, even among those whose abhorrence of treachery was outstanding, there was a marked distinction made between those who betrayed their own people – that is, their own country – and those nationals of other nations who infiltrated an alien country for purposes of espionage. Mercy could be extended to the latter, who were, after all enemy-aliens but it could not be extended to the former. Treason had been, in those earlier times, a completely despicable, totally inexcusable crime, when committed by a man or a woman, against their own people.

A fey woman of that 1914 cataclysm, Mata Hari, survived the war in spirit more successfully than all the heroes, if biographies were any gauge, even though she actually accomplished practically nothing as a spy, and with each utterance confirmed a suspicion, that, both emotionally and intellectually, she had ceased to develop after the age of eight, although her other development was adequate.

She was a woman, not exactly an unheard of coincidence in the annals of either espionage or treachery, and during her brief tenure – she was executed as a spy by the French – she made capital use of an ample physical endowment during an age when modesty forbade equally as endowed women from appearing as she did, in filmy 'harem' pantaloons, and a pair of insufficient breastcups. She was not among the illustrious female spies of history. But she did epitomise something – the glamour of treachery among the sophisticates who scorned the old virtues.

Decades after her death she continued to be eulogized in songs, in books, in motion picutres, as the tragic heroine. She gradually paled, of course, but what Mati Hari had really epitomized was more than tragedy. She exemplified the glamour of immorality, of deceit, stupidity, and egotistic treachery. She was representative of a new era; she was the prototype of a fresh, exalted variety of people to whom the stab in the back was entirely respectable; people to whom the old virtues were ludicrous.

She left her bones among those other bones, over eight million individual sets of them, to enrichen the depleted soil of France, after 1914, adding with her mote to the unfolding new epoch an entire host of things which she had helped towards a common acceptance, which, up to the year of the Diamond Jubilee, had been considered inexcusable.

The values changed, the tempo increased, the subtleties proliferated, as the sail, the horse and the empires yielded after so many generations to the internal combustion engine, as well as to the headlong rush of time and all the ill-omened changes that time's flight presaged.

Pan-Germanism sparked the new impetus, and pan-Germanism sustained it. German recovery from the devastating losses of the First World War – over 1,700,000 German lives, catastrophic ruin in city after city, complete economic prostration – was extremely swift. In 1897 it would have been thought impossible. Yet in one decade the recovery was massively under way, and all that terrible sacrifice had not shaken the German thrust called *lebensraum*.

Two decades after the thunderous collapse of imperial Germany, Teutonic fleets, arms, ideals, were instilling fresh dread in foreign hearts. German vigour and dedication were supporting experimentation among the new factors, all based upon *Blitz*, speed: first-strike strategy, total mechanisation, sustained assault, massive use of the air, concerted use of the underside of the sea – and the 'big lie', propaganda on such a scale, employed with such boldness, such ceaseless impact, that even those who knew the truth were struck mute before the skilful panegyric.

Nothing remained of those earlier times. Even the old conviction that no nation could survive constant combat was proved wrong. To those who said, after 1914, that the First World War had drained the substance of Germany and that another world war would destroy civilisation, Germany's new imperialist, speaking sincerely, *in foro conscientiae*, told the world that it was "eternal peace" which destroyed people, and *Der Führer* hurried his revived nation down the road, where he said, only the fittest survived, and that neither the individual nor society could escape this natural decree, which he then proceeded to implement.

1,700,000 dead Germans had not resulted in a loss of fibre. Total economic prostration had not drained Germany's substance. All these levelled cities and mounds of flattened rubble were not irredeemable. In less than half the time that England had required to mount the Industrial Revolution, the New Germany, *imperium in imperio*, was again the land of marcher lords.

One thing remained: The conviction that, even were it a

desirable accomplishment, no strong nation could be vanquished with haste; it was not possible to reduce a civilized citadel of vast cities, great culture, historic traditions, overnight. It could not be done; it had never been done.

It was done. Follow the sequence: on 15th March 1939, Germany invaded Czechoslovakia, overrunning and conquering the country in a matter of days. On 22nd March 1939, Germany overran Lithuania, destroying the sovereignty of that nation in one day. On 1st September, at 04.55 hours, Germany invaded Poland, a country with three million men under arms and a heritage going back in culture in art and science many centuries, conquering that land in seventeen days. On 9th April 1940, Germany struck at Norway, and despite savage resistance conquered that nation in twenty-one days. Denmark fell in one day.

German arms conquered the Netherlands in four days, and overran Belgium and Luxemberg. Belgium capitulated on the eighteenth day, Luxemberg did not stand half that long. On 5th June 1940, Germany hurled its power against France, on an arc from Sedan to Abbeville, and France, a seat of European culture, of leadership, of enormous power and prestige, with vast resources, a great navy and a large army, lasted exactly eighteen days, from 5th June to 22nd June 1940, being able to stand only as long as had much smaller Belgium.

Thus passed the last vestige, and the last conviction, of an earlier time when warfare was conducted differently, by men who almost invariable acted from principle – right or wrong – but who anathematised such men as Bonaparte because they were gamblers, which the oldtime professionals were not, except occasionally in the tactical sense.

Between 15th March 1939 and 22nd June 1940, that final conviction, a complete anachronism by 1939, which categorically held no strong nation could be conquered rapidly, fell as the final fatality. There was never again to be a leisurely approach to anything, certainly not to warfare, and not to everyday living, either. Not to education, not even to sports. Henceforth speed counted, nothing less, and as history is a thicket of paradoxes, in passing it can do no harm to note that although the Germans capitalized on the *Blitz* principal, contrary to common belief they did not originate it, that distinction belonged to a small group of Britons, among them the late B.H. Liddell Hart. These military theorists worked out on paper the precise tactics adopted by Germany, and in fact, the Britons compared their new strategy to lightning, a designation which the Germans also borrowed, calling the new strategy *'Blitzkrieg'*, lightning war.

1914-1918 was a prelude. 1939-1945 was a confirmation. In the former era it was *"Deutschland über alles"*, intimating that the old pride of Imperial Germany still lived. But by 1939 there was as ringing a cry, but no longer founded on pride, no longer rooted in civilized tradition, and no longer a corollary with any of the earlier sentiments. It was simply *"Und willst du nicht Genosse sein, so schlagen wir den Schädel ein!"* It was the statement of the New Germany; wherever Germans went, so also went that dictum. It was an epitome of the reversion to the ancient Teutonic ethos of National Socialist (Nazi) Germany, which was, as observed above, *Imperium in imperio*, a state within a state – that is, Nazi Germany was still Germany. The new dictum was straight from the heart of tribal Germany. It went back over a thousand years, over 2000 years, to the chanted shouts of Germania at the gates of Rome, and from that time forward it was the most feared of all outcries from west-central Europe.

When its protagonists overran Europe, beginning in 1939, it was the only rational way to explain their behaviour, in Germany, as well as in the conquered lands. Odin and the Valkyries had replaced Luther, von Spee, and Speyer, the new German National Church of Nazi Alfred Rosenberg freed all Germans of the old religious and ethical concepts, replacing these with absolute neo-heathenistic doctrines. Might alone became right. Power alone was authority, and extremism in the defence of both was the solemn duty of Germans. *"Und willst du nicht Genosse sein, so schlagen wir den Schädel ein!"*

"And if you will not join with us, we'll crack your skull!"

2

"We Have Been Defeated"

10th May 1940, when the Germans unleashed their first thrust, hastily reinforced Allied strength was equal in all ways but one – comprehension. In less than a month the British were gone, evacuated in haste at Dunkirk, the Dutch, Belgian, and the best of the French forces, were overrun, decimated, hammered into a dumb-show effort that was slashed to threads. Germany's triumphant *Wehrmacht*, 120 divisions, faced all that remained, a stunned, confused Allied host of sixty five divisions.

Thor's hammer struck in three directions. A German army drove hard from the west, a second army came from the east against the 'invincible' Maginot Line. The third blow came when von Runstedt crossed the Aisne, and within three days Heinz Guderian's panzers were through the French defences at Chalon, racing southward. By 12th June French efforts were collapsing. German motorized elements spread out in all directions, unchecked. Two days before, on 10th June, the French government had fled Paris. On the 12th Paris was declared an open city. On 14th June the Germans hung their war-banners on the Eiffel Tower and the Arc de Triomphe. On 15th June Britain's new Prime Minister, successor to Neville Chamberlain, who resigned on 10th May, was roused from bed at about half-past seven by a telephone call to London from the French Premier, Paul Reynaud, successor to Chamberlain's French counterpart, Edouard Deladier. Premier Reynaud, in office not quite three months, speaking in English, said to Winston Churchill, "We have been defeated. . . . We are beaten; we have lost the battle."

Two days later France asked its conquerors for a truce, and on 25th June the last battle ended.

Winston Churchill, well into his sixties by 1940, an individual whose impressions were mostly from those earlier times, those more leisurely decades, wrote later: "Of course this picture [of a fallen France] presented a general impression of defeat. I had seen a good deal of this sort of thing in the previous war, and the idea of the line being broken, even on a broad front, did not convey to my mind the appalling consequences that now flowed from it. . . . I did not comprehend the violence of the revolution effected since the last war by the incursion of a mass of fast-moving heavy armour."

Neither, evidently, had any of the other European leaders, until it was too late for most. Churchill, however, had two great advantages. The first was his ability to recover from the shock, and the second advantage was that the Germans halted at the English Channel, not entirely because they chose to. Exulting in their unprecedented triumphs, many Germans wanted to storm across to Britain. They had smashed their way through the European heartland, had demolished the myth of Polish and French power, and were now actually on the Channel Islands. Twenty-one miles of water were all that kept them from an English beach-head; they had crossed five times that much hostile countryside in a day.

But they never got across. Historically, Caesar's oversight had culminated in Caesar's defeat. Britain was more vulnerable to the new-style war than she had been in 1066, or earlier, when the Danes came. She was in a comparable condition, in the spring and summer of 1940, to her condition in 54 B.C. when Julius Caesar's second invasion made strong inroads. She could have been defeated in 1940. She could not have been defeated only one year later. Given the time, after 1940, to marshal resources, to glean from friends and allies, to organize and harass, and to eventually compel the Germans to defend themselves, Britain's unshakeable resolution made possible a revival of hope. But as a process it was painfully slow, and meanwhile the Germans turned inward to the task of organising *Festung Europa*, their Europe, so that all its wealth and divergent resources could be funnelled into depots for the German war machine. It was an enormous task, even without the gnat's sting from across the Channel, which ultimately became a lion's bite.

For a while after the collapse of France there was a lull. *Der Führer* visited the capital of his new colony, Paris. Marshal Petain, a career defeatist, replaced Paul Reynaud as Premier, and established the government of unoccupied France at Vichy, under the aegis of Pierre Laval, one of the least admirable of the Vichy French. Charles de Gaulle, subsequent leader of French resistance, fled to England, and the soldiers of the *Reich* rested – their stunning accomplishments already passing into history.

For a time now it would be Germany's organisers and administrators who would create order from chaos, and this was to prove the most difficult of all accomplishments; there were remnants of the defeated armies everywhere. Pockets of resistance existed. Secret cliques of saboteurs flourished. It was dangerous for individual members of the *Wehrmacht* to appear, even in broad daylight. If the idea was to Teutonize the French, as the Caesars had Romanized Gaul almost two thousand years earlier, the effort was doomed to fail, because France by 1940, was a highly civilized state, where the ancient tribesmen of Gaul had been ripe for social improvement.

Even among the civilians of France there was virulent resistance, and as German requirements made deeper inroads in all areas, including those of agriculture and food processing, an increasingly gaunt populace settled into the categories which commonly afflict a conquered people.

There were the collaborators, sustained by a conviction that Germany would triumph over embattled Britain. There were the apathetic, largely opportunistic, for whom the future was obscure and unimportant, and to whom day by day existence was paramount. There were also those to whom resistance was a duty, and these people could, and did, exert a great influence over the second largest group, the apathetic, until each increase of defiance from Britain, each humiliation of the conquerors, heightened a general feeling that there was hope. Then, the occupation of all the vanquished lands became a nightmare for the Germans. But throughout the long autumn of 1940, Britain was engrossed at home with a multiplicity of dilemmas arising from an unprecedented confusion – there were 13,600 French naval personnel encamped at one place, 5,530 French troops at Trentham Park, homeless French warships cluttering British seaports, Dutch, Norwegian, Polish remnants, sailors, soldiers, airmen, and clamouring generals, adding to the burden of home defence. The Germans of Europe got the respite they needed, and, already convinced of their superiority and invincibility, they reacted to resistance with the barbarity identical to that which their ancient forefathers had used against Rome.

The result was that the horror of Germany's extermination and exploitation system, to a great degree kept secret from the rest of the world prior to the conquest of Europe, was fed such hordes of vanquished people that it expanded into a state industry, complete with immense crematoriums – and secrecy was no longer possible. Nor, in fact, was it even desirable, to a great many Germans, on the grounds that dread of a conqueror was the surest way to achieve, if not outright co-operation, then at least submission. And of course, this was true to some extent, but among the conquered French the depth of hatred for the conqueror ran deep and ran strong. All the French loathed their conquerors, but not all Frenchmen were willing to risk their lives to prove it, and as the summer of defeat ran along towards the autumn of 1940 the apathy deepened. Immediate succour was demanded, and Britain, under threat of land attack, increasingly battered by bombers from across the Channel, short of everything which was needed to wage this kind of a war, huddled on her island with only one worthwhile ally left – the United States – and that ally, ponderously slow to move, could not offer immediate succour, except through harrassment, while she meanwhile strained every sinew towards an achievement of the larger perspective. Thus the French were left adrift with their shock and apathy, and smouldering hatred.

Reactions of course varied, but a central theme of hatred lay beneath the behaviour of all but a small percentage of the French. The divisions which had previously flourished, as between leftists and rightists, still existed, and as time passed they would create problems; but after the fall there was only

The German. Even collaborators, and of course the
supposedly neutral Vichy French, who were never very
successfully neutral, hated their conquerors. Of that small
percentage who evinced no outward animus, and who were
motivated by almost any sentiment except those rooted in
honour or ethics, it could be said that they were no better or
worse before the fall. But they were a very real danger after the
fall. Small though they may have been in numbers,
nonetheless it was through them that the Germans were able
to achieve their most spectacular apprehensions of
underground resistance numbers.

The law of retribution ultimately corrected this, but not in
time to save a great many of the French from execution, and as
the lull continued, as the French recovered from the shock,
and as humiliation and degradation fed their rancour, they
turned increasingly to resistance. For the individual, the
summer of 1940 was a time of stunned incomprehension, but
by autumn and winter that had passed. Then it became
individually imperative to choose, as it always has for the
individual, what course to pursue in the face of drastically
altered circumstances. Sabotage ensued, of course, and
repeatedly stung the conquerors, who were striving by night
as well as by day to marshal the resources of Europe to sustain
their next strike, which was to be against Russia.

German retaliation was savage. Unable, in many instances
to capture the actual perpetrators, innocent people were
rounded up and kept, like cattle, to be executed when
sabotage was committed. But as a deterrent, this was never
very successful. Collaboration with Britain or de Gaulle's free
French forces did not have to be proved, it only had to be
suspected, to qualify the individual for prompt execution.

There was at this time, practically no co-ordinated espionage
between France and Britain. Even co-operation at the
embryonic level of the loosely-organised saboteur
organisations was minimal. Britain was almost completely
occupied with accumulating the means for achieving re-entry
to the Continent, and rightly so; no war was won by blowing
up railroad bridges or by ambushing squads of an enemy. But
these methods of harrassment were all that was left to the

French, so they turned more and more to employing them.

Gradually, individual names of people unheard of before the war, began to assume a certain, usually a local or regional, prominence. Without leaders in France, the French were evolving their own leaders, but these were quite often inexperienced, sometimes even foolish, or naïve people. They were caught in droves; the fortunate ones were jailed in France, the unfortunate ones were entrained for Germany, there to perish under almost unbelievable circumstances in such places as Auschwitz, Ravensbruck, Buchenwald, and the complex of Neuengamme.

The circumstances which encouraged this evolution of resistance was devoid of an adequate screening process. It was also devoid of a precedent, so perhaps much that ensued was excusable. Training was done in the field. Selectivity was based on willingness, not skill. Emotion almost invariably over-rode every other consideration, and the result was that the *Résistance* of France was shot through with people whose qualifications for sabotage and, eventually, espionage, were woefully inadequate, and these people served beside others who, also without training, became in time, when they managed to survive, some of the best *résistants* of the war.

The French *résistant* needed more than courage and cunning. There was the absolute certainty of what would follow discovery and capture. It required a quite different variety of courage to mine a bridge stealthily at night, or to establish an ambush from hiding, than was required in the bright light of day, to contemplate the certainty of physical torture and ultimate execution if one were caught. Not all *résistants* were endowed with the latter kind of courage, but the tragedy was that, until these lesser people were caught, and subsequently interrogated under torture, their comrades had no way of knowing who might betray them.

The circumstances were indeed without precedent for the French. Before the new year of 1941 was very far advanced, they learned a great many harsh lessons. But they persevered – the courageous as well as the potential jackals, the unskilled but dedicated, the fools, the weaklings who were able to conceal their weakness, the reckless along with the savagely murderous – a great coterie of largely dissimilar people sometimes willingly concerting their efforts, just as often refusing to associate with one another, but functioning with an increasing malevolence against a common enemy, most often in ways the Germans could not successfully anticipate nor prevent.

The matter of personalities was always uppermost. There was no military discipline among those early *résistants*, except on the squad-level, and even then it obtained only during clandestine undertakings. *Résistants* were individuals first, saboteurs second. Nor were they always men. In fact they did not appear at times even to be predominantly men, which was perhaps a good thing, for when Britain's Special Operations Executive, and other espionage and sabotage establishments ultimately joined the *Résistance*, supporting, arming and equipping it, there were many women agents in the field.

But among the French *Résistance*, in those days of blood and ash, one particular name earned a degree of notoriety which enabled it to be remembered when an entire host of other names had been forgotten – Mathilde Carré.

3

Belard-Carré

Madame Belard, from a middle-class family of the Jura, was delivered of a daughter at Chateauroux, 19th February, 1910, a matter of concern to her husband, who was a consulting engineer, because his wife was no longer a girl; they already had a grown up son, who was shortly to begin a martial career, *via* the military college of St Cyr.

But Madame had no difficulty; the baby girl was small, robust, and delightfully appealing. She had very dark hair, green eyes, and the stocky physique of many French girls and women. She was christened Mathilde. As Mathilde Belard grew, she developed a quick smile and a lively, gay and pleasant personality. She was the child of her parents' late years; she was spoiled, of course, and she became headstrong. In the family she was called Lily.

In some ways Mathilde Belard was difficult to know, for while she made friends easily, all her life there was a streak of something extravagant in her character that kept her slightly apart. She was companionable at the same time she was very competitive. She formed powerful attachments, as a child, and just as suddenly abandoned them. She was not pretty, but as she matured she became very attractive, physically. She was not tall, but she was solid and vibrant. She became the kind of girl, in her teens, boys stared at. And not just boys. But she avoided entanglements, was never involved in gossip or scandal, did not go to dances or parties, and in fact attended the Sorbonne, acquiring a degree in Law, at a time when serious education for girls was considered a waste of time and certainly so in the case of an abundantly endowed girl such as Mathilde Belard.

She was headstrong, and she was entirely aware of her impression on men. But if she lacked depth, Mathilde Belard

did not lack a conviction that her lot in life was destined to
achieve a remarkable influence, and in this her wilful mother
had a part. Like most French of her class Madame Belard's
ambition for her children was practically boundless, and with
her son well launched on his military career there remained
the consideration of her daughter's career.

But as Mathilde matured, her headstrong individuality
clashed with Madame Belard's wilfulness. She made her own
decisions; they were not always wise, and because Mathilde
had a capacity for fierce jealousy, they were also quite often
reckless and vindictive decisions.

Madame Belard had visions of an exemplary marriage for
her daughter, but when voluptuous Mathilde was in her
twenties she brought a young school teacher named Carré
home to meet her parents, and Madame Belard's fantasies
collapsed. Neither she nor Mathilde's father made a secret of
their disappointment. Schoolmasters were not good marraige
prospects. They did not make much money. Their lives were
unexciting and cloistered.

The Belards did not openly oppose the match, but they
persisted in downgrading its possibilities, eventually
managing to sow enough doubt in Mathilde's mind, so that
when the schoolmaster asked her to marry him – he had just
secured a position at Oran, in Algeria, a romantic-sounding
place – she had to reach a decision. Mathilde resolved this
crisis by rolling a pair of dice. The dice came up in favour of
marriage.

Mathilde Belard became Mathilde Belard Carré in
September, 1933, the same year Adolf Hitler's use of the
Reichstag fire in Berlin sent his National Socialism into
soaring popularity throughout Germany. She and her
husband went to Oran, a drowsy, hot town; in 1933, a dusty
outpost of the French empire. In Algeria Mathilde mitigated
some of the boredom by accepting a position as school
teacher, and, with her husband, became part of the French
colonial social fabric in a place where imagination and
initiative were stultified as much by a stratified social
existence as by the heat.

Nevertheless, voluptuous Mathilde Carré's marriage,

despite its unique founding on a roll of dice, worked rather well
for six years, which was a record not achieved by many
marriages more substantially based. But she wanted children,
and the first blow came when it was discovered that her
husband was unable to provide her with any.

The second blow came in the sixth year of her marriage
when her mother-in-law confided that her husband's father
had died in a mental institution. It was the shock of this
revelation, and the fact that her husband had concealed it
from her, that occasioned the serious alienation which
henceforth marked Mathilde's relationship with her husband.

Finally, with the glamour gone, with the disillusionment
established, Oran itself began to pall. The quiet, monotonous
existence in French North Africa finally began to militate
against the robust vitality of this very physical, very vital
Frenchwoman of twenty-nine, who could see age coming upon
her stealthily in that dull place, while elsewhere great events
were beginning to take form.

She filed for divorce the year war came, and her husband
was called up as a commissioned officer and sent to Syria
exactly six years, to the month, from the time he and Mathilde
were married. They would only meet once again, a very
painful encounter for him, his love as strong as ever. He was
killed shortly after that last meeting, while fighting in Italy.

With her husband gone and Europe in flames, Mathilde
Carré left Algeria for Marseilles. Upon arriving in France she
went, first, to the apartment of her parents on the Avenue des
Gobelins, in Paris, then she volunteered to serve as a nurse in
the corps of the French Red Cross.

It was the first real release for Mathilde Carré in a very long
time. She was always robust, vital, energetic. She was
enthusiastic about her new vocation, which was fortunate,
because by the time she had completed her training and was
posted to a hospital outside Paris, the Nazi meat-grinder was
keeping French hospital trains constantly rolling to the rear
areas with maimed soldiers.

But the real battle of France had not yet started, so
Mathilde was allowed enough time to be prepared. She
excelled; she always strove to excel. She worked very long

hours for great lengths of time, and although she nearly
fainted the first time she was called upon to assist in surgery,
she eventually became inured to all the unnerving sights. In
late April of 1940 she was ordered to a forward hospital on the
eastern front, near the Maginot Line. She arrived there in
early May. On the 10th, German armour began its drive
across the Lowlands. Streams of battered refugees streaming
into France, along with wounded Allied soldiers, filled the
hospital. Mathilde's vitality was put to its most severe test.
She worked almost without respite, amply demonstrating yet
again, that under the kind of stress she was presently being
subjected to, in which she was called upon to give
unrestrictedly of herself, she was entirely willing and capable.

Subsequently, with the overwhelming impact of total war
sweeping into France, she was again transferred. This time to
the hospital at Beauvais, where again her indomitable vitality
earned her praise, recognition, and a military citation.

The unleashed fury of Germany's armed thrust was
sweeping everything before it. Both civilian and military
hospitals were full, and the injured continued to stream in.
Also, the orderly processes began breaking down. Aerial
attacks by Germany's dreaded *Stukas* made rail as well as road
transport almost impossible; many hospitals exhausted their
medical supplies and were unable to rely on the arrival of fresh
supplies.

Often, in the wake of bombing attacks, the gravely injured
could not be brought to hospitals and had to be treated where
they lay. Mathilde went out with doctors on a number of these
calls and at least once was compelled to take shelter in a
bomb crater when a flight of *Stuka* dive-bombers came in for a
strike. Her subsequent comment about this experience was
that, in moments of great personal peril, a person's entire
being responded with almost sexual anticipation.

The German onslaught never slackened. Opposition to it
disintegrated on all fronts. In the pockets where Allied troops
still resisted after the German advance swept past, the
stationary defenders were obliterated from the air.

It all happened too fast. As communications broke down
demoralisation set in. Mathilde Carré became a refugee

among refugees hastening towards Paris. She had her military citation attesting to her courage and capability, but on the road to Paris she was surrounded by gaunt soldiers with grander decorations, and they too were in flight.

In Paris, she visited her parents at the apartment on the Avenue des Gobelins, shared their shock and anxiety with them, joined in their prayers for her soldier brother, then was ordered to the hospital at Orleans, seventy five miles southwest of Paris. As a child she had attended a girls' school there, for a short time. The city was familiar to her, but not as it now was, full of terrible rumours and fear. There were the usual refugees, but not nearly as many as she had encountered at Beauvais, which had been on the direct route of the German thrust through the Somme. But the demoralisation had spread this far, and with reason; the first time Orleans had seen Germans, Attila had besieged it, again in 1870 the Germans came, and that time they occupied Orleans. Joan of Arc was its patroness, and although it was older than France itself, Orleans was vulnerable, if the Germans reached Paris. But for a short while, at any rate, a matter of days actually, the physically indomitable, abundantly provocative Frenchwoman with the large, near-sighted green eyes, had a respite.

Work at the hospital was, as always, intense and demanding, but at least in Orleans, as France struggled frantically elsewhere to avoid collapse, Mathilde Carré had little moments to herself for relaxation.

During one of these little interludes she encountered a soldier, a lieutenant of the 49th Tank Battalion, whom she had known as a child in Jura, René Aubertin. Their renewed friendship was necessarily brief. The lieutenant, like all the other soldiers reaching Orleans, was passing through, and as the German advance swept closer to Paris, the more Orleans filled up with confused hordes of both soldiers and refugee civilians. To encounter a childhood friend during a moment of respite was a bitter-sweet coincidence, as the skies over France grew steadily darker.

Finally, Orleans was caught in the respite. Refugees streamed through, leaderless soldiers arrived, local people fled as the Germans bored ruthlessly towards Paris. Mathilde's hospital was evacuated. She was issued an order to reach Bordeaux on the west coast, the Bay of Biscay, half the length of France from Orleans,without being told how this was to be accomplished, as France's transportation system, like her government, failed.

Without panic, but totally unprepared, Mathilde was loaned a room in one of the great homes beyond Orleans by a tank element of the French Army which was billeted there, and a few days later she managed to secure a place to huddle in the bed of a French army lorry, already over-loaded with other refugees.

Now, finally, the Germans arrived – in *Stukas*, dive-bombing the clogged roads, strafing the sheep-like endless queues of people; old men harnessed to carts in which rode old women, young women holding tightly to the hands of small children, their men with one of the beaten armies of France. She reached Toulouse, well south of Bordeaux and inland, on the route of escape in the direction of Spain by way of the Pyrenees. Here, she heard there was an Englishman who would arrange escape to Britain, and went at once to find him. He was an English officer, and in fact he was helping as much as he could, but his advice to the sturdy, little, green-eyed Frenchwoman with the military decoration was not to abandon France, but to stay and give aid.

The German victory was complete. The dreaded dive-bombers no longer attacked, and although German mechanized columns appeared everywhere, spreading through France on pacification duty, there was no longer heavy fighting. After a while there was no fighting at all. And the stillness was in many ways worse than the tumult.

Mathilde Carré was as footloose, as much in limbo, as any other French refugee. She was not, however, as lacking in resourcefulness, nor as bewildered and helpless. She had been looking after the welfare of Mathilde Carré for many years. She continued to do so. France was a conquered country, well, as she said one time, "What was to be done?" And the answer, clearly, was to survive.

Toulouse was crowded beyond expectation. There were also refugees who passed through in the night, seeking to

rendezvous with a Basque or a Spaniard in order to reach
Spain. The Germans had long lists of wanted men and
women. The French army was disbanded, which was largely a
formality, and that fact increased the southward flow, too.
Mathilde acquired a friend, a young woman about her own
age. They managed. Others might sleep in alleys and fields,
and huddle in bewilderment, Mathilde and her friend visited
the crowded, noisy cafés. They flirted a little, and one evening
at a particular cafe, Mathilde saw a familiar face, but now
René Aubertin was no longer in uniform. Also, the very brief
encounter at Orleans had left a number of topics under
discussion unsatisfactorily concluded. The friendship was
resumed. In those days there were compelling forces to bring
people together, foremost of course was survival, but in France
there was also the healthy hatred. People could not forget, the
daily radio broadcasts did not allow them to forget, who was
the master of France.

For a while people did nothing. It was enough, for a short
while, to simply try and understand what had happened. To
visit the cafés, to discuss the events of the past few weeks, to
attempt a reasonable assessment because, clearly, someone
had made a terrible blunder. And of course, as the numbness
passed, to make plans. It was impossible to exist without
plans.

One October evening Mathilde Carré met a man in one of
the cafés, a Pole with half the look of a gypsy; dark hair, large,
dark eyes, lean build and lithe movements. His name was
Roman Czerniawski. There were in France at this time a
rather large number of Poles who had escaped their own
country after its conquest by the Germans, and who had
reached France to carry on the war. But this particular Pole
was unique in several ways, as Mathilde Carré discovered. At
the outbreak of the war Roman Czerniawski had been
assigned as Chief Intelligence Officer of the First Polish
Division. Captain Czerniawski was just under thirty years of
age. In November of 1939, not quite two months after the
German invasion of Poland and its subsequent collapse,
Captain Czerniawski, (later Wing Commander) whose First
Polish Division had been fighting in France alongside the 20th

French Army Corps, not only looked more French than Polish, but was in fact passing as a Frenchman with the best of all affadavits; a genuine French passport.

Czerniawski's unit was fighting in Alsace when Marshal Petain signed the surrender agreement. In the mass confusion which ensued, and which to a large extent immediately preceeded this event, a large number of Poles were evacuated to Britain. But there were also quite a number of Poles who, literally, missed the boat. Roman Czerniawski was one of the latter. So was a friend of his, a former member of Czerniawski's staff, Lieutenant Bernard Krutki, in civil life a doctor of languages at Poznan University. Czerniawski was fluent in Polish and French, but Bernard Krutki was fluent in Russian, English, Italian, Spanish, German and French.

Another Pole who missed the evacuation was a former staff officer to General Sikorski, commander-in-chief of Polish forces in France. His name was Colonel Vincent Zarembski. And while General Sikorski became head of the Polish government in exile in London, Colonel Zaremski, like Captain Czerniawski, remained in France.

When France surrendered, Captain Czerniawski's element of the 1st Division was encamped in the Vosges, near Lunéville. Here, Czerniawski met a young French widow, Reneé Borni, at that time employed at a Lunéville hotel. This meeting coincided with Czerniawski's capture by the Germans. He escaped, Reneé Borni hid him, and when the fall of France ensued, Reneé gave Roman Czerniawski her late husband's clothes, and his passport – his identity. The similarity was close enough, and in fact the clothes fitted perfectly. She also gave him much more, before he left the Vosges, travelling southwest towards the Spanish border, and although his safety was directly the result of the passionate attachment of Reneé Borni, the somewhat dull-witted widow of Lunéville, Roman Czerniawski did not mention any of this to Mathilde Carré. He did tell her of being taken near Lunéville by the Germans, and of escaping. He also told her of his connection with Polish Intelligence, and of course, since women were Roman Czerniawski's weakness, he made love to her, which, at this juncture in her life, when she was at a loose

end with none of the attachments most women require,
Mathilde Carré responded with all the ardour of her nature,
and that, according to the record, was considerable; she was
described by a man who knew her well in the years ahead, as a
"dangerous nymphomaniac". Roman Czerniawski, who
survived the war, left behind no complaints of this period of his
life.

Mathilde said of him that he reminded her of a spoiled
child, and she liked that. Evidently there was nothing about
Roman Czerniawski she did not like. They became practically
inseparable, the energetic, voluptuous, green-eyed French
woman with the complex character, and the equally energetic
but less complex Polish Intelligence officer masquerading as
one Armand Borni.

In some ways their new-found companionship was based
upon identical factors. Of course they shared a deep antipathy
for the Germans. Beyond that, they both had considerable
vanity, both also had a high estimation of their personal worth
and intelligence, and both were romantics at a time when life
was very real and very hazardous.

Where they differed the most was in the depth and scope of
their emotions. Czerniawski was steadfast, loyal, and to some
degree fatalistic. Mathilde's moods, like her sentiments, were
extravagant. She could not love Czerniawski, she had to
possess him. She could not hate Germans, she had to despise
them, and somewhere, just beyond the blinding flash of these
exhausting emotions, they of course fused for Lily Carré,
exactly as those other extravagant emotions, deadly fear and
sensuality, had fused that time she had been under personal
attack by *Stukas*, back at Beauvais in the Oise.

She called him 'Toto' and he called her 'Spitfire', and as
France gradually recovered, slowly adjusted to the
unthinkable, Mathilde Carré and Roman Czerniawski
affirmed their attachment to the extent that he confided in her
that he knew of a Polish underground organisation in
Marseilles which was seeking to effect an accord with London.
He also told her that what was needed in France was a large-
scale underground organization capable of supplying London
with detailed, current, and absolutely reliable information

on everything from French morale to German activities.

But, as a matter of fact, General Sikorski's former staff officer, Colonel Zaremski was already in the process of organizing such a group in Toulouse, called 'Tudor'. This espionage-sabotage *réseaux* eventually completed a network which included Marseilles, Lyons, ancient Clermont-Ferrand, and even Vichy. Czerniawski was aware of this, but what he had in mind was a new organization, with contacts in other towns, and areas, of France. Nor was he either alone in this projection, nor original in the concept of a widespread espionage network in France, functioning for, and of course financed by, London. But at the moment, when he confided in Mathilde Carré, she, at least, with no knowledge of espionage, thought it was an heroic concept. With her customary over-reaction she agreed to co-operate wholeheartedly, this very physical, small woman with the wide knowledge of France, and with her equally broad acquaintanceship with dozens of people from one end of the country to the other. She very accurately described her reactions, later, when she said, ". . . the whole world and the victory of the world seemed to be in our hands. Life with Toto had wings. I did not know what I was doing but I had complete faith in him. . .".

They decided to make the journey to Paris and create their organization in the very heart of France, which was now also the nerve-centre of the Occupation, but first, Czerniawski had in mind visiting the underground at Marseilles, which was always a hotbed of intrigue, even when there was no Occupation. He also had in mind sending Mathilde to Vichy to glean as much information as she could from the factions there, which included pro-Germans, pro-Gaullists, pro-British, and even pro-Vichyites.

Mathilde was elated. She once more had a purpose in her life. She and her Toto ". . . embraced . . . and danced for joy in the room of our hotel". They went about creating an espionage network with more enthusiasm than practical common sense, but in their favour was the condition of France at this time. Even those who had cautiously adopted an attitude of mild optimism were being disillusioned; the Germans ruled with an iron fist. Their ruthlessness alienated even the few French,

such as Pierre Laval, who had begun to have hope, subsequent
to the surrender, that existence under the swastika might in
time become bearable. A contrary condition obtained, and
more of the French than ever loathed their conquerors. This
situation helped the Polish officer and his green-eyed co-
conspirator immeasurably, and at least for the naïve Lily
Carré the subsequent visit to Vichy was a great help, for in
Vichy she got her first instructions in espionage, a very
dangerous vocation at any time, but in an occupied country,
under the very noses – and ears – of its conquerors, also a very
deadly vocation.

4
La Chatte et Armand

Czerniawski went to Marseilles and Mathilde went to Vichy, that very insubstantial area of France euphemistically called 'Unoccupied France', where one of the Gestapo's senior officers in France had a residence nearly opposite the residence of Marshal Petain.

While Czerniawski was familiarizing himself with the underground activities in Marseilles, Mathilde cultivated a number of pro-Gaullist officers of the French Intelligence bureau, the *Deuxième*, in Vichy. Her personality as well as her physical attractiveness were a great help. There were also a number of American newsmen in Vichy, roughly a year before the United States would enter the war, and from the latter Mathilde Carré acquired a broad understanding of world conditions while from the former, particularly two enthusiastic French officers, Simmoneau and Achard, whom she allowed to believe she was also a Gaullist, she received instructions in basic espionage, including terminology, designations, methods of coding and delivering information. It was here, at the Hotel Ambassadeurs, that Mathilde Carré was first called 'The Cat'. American newsmen gave her the name. They called her 'Our Little Black Cat'. The French intelligence officers called her the 'Little Persian Cat'. This was henceforth to be the code-name of Mathilde Carré: the Cat.

When she returned to Toulouse, Czerniawski liked the sobriquet and that confirmed its adoption. He had also been using the given name of the man whose French identity he had assumed, Armand, and because in the future he was to be referred to by that name in all communications, coded and otherwise, henceforth herein, Roman Czerniawski will be known as Armand.

They were now ready to leave Toulouse and take up residence in Paris, where the establishment of their *réseau* was to be undertaken. But an awkward embarrassment intruded for Mathilde: Her husband suddenly appeared.

Lieutenant Carré was still in service with the fighting French, but after more than a year of hard service he was a different man, leaner, more distraught, not at all confident that the France he had been fighting for could survive. He wanted Mathilde, whom he called Lily, to return with him to the comparative safety of North Africa. For Lieutenant Carré, it was a cry from the heart; he wanted, at least to try, to turn back the clock to a time when he had been safe, had been loved, and been a resident of a sane world.

Mathilde did not give him an outright refusal. She said she would first have to make the journey to Paris for some personal things she had left with her parents. Simultaneously, she told Armand she would get rid of this nuisance of a man. She then suggested to Lieutenant Carré that, since he was clearly exhausted and in need of rest, he should visit the countryside beyond Toulouse and relax until she returned from Paris. Then, she and Armand, of whom Lieutenant Carré knew nothing, entrained for Paris and lost themselves, which was not a difficult thing to do in a city which covered thirty square miles, had a population of about three million souls, which did not include thousands of Germans who would have been delighted to encounter a member of the fighting Free French forces.

Lieutenant Carré waited, and when he could wait no longer, he left, but he wrote letters, many of which were returned, unclaimed. He never heard from his wife again. Later, he was killed during the Allied invasion of Italy, at Cassino, but by that time Mathilde had divorced him.

Elsewhere, events in Europe, throughout the world, were creating conditions which would ultimately alter the favourable balance of power for the Germans. One of them was the American reaction to the *Luftwaffe's* ceaseless pounding of Britain from the skies, in wave after wave of indiscriminate bombing attacks which levelled churches, schools, even hospitals and homes for the aged.

The United States commitment was already considerable, but the indiscriminate killing of civilians in Britain, together with tales of German atrocities on the Continent, increased the average American's antipathy towards the Axis powers, and that of course was an omen for the future which would eventually work against Germany. Additionally, Germany's announcement of a total sea blockade around the British Isles, at a time when aid in significant amounts could only reach Britain by sea, further antagonized those, including the United States, who were attempting in varying degrees to ameliorate the island's hardships.

The Soviet Union also, which was Germany's ally in the rape of Poland, and which profited considerably from the subsequent Balkan confusion, began to have second thoughts about its Nazi associates, and towards the winter of 1940, began systematically to take precautionary measures. Germany's sweeping triumphs of 1939 and early 1940, were, by the winter of 1940 and the early spring of 1941, beginning to feel the effects of the slowly-accumulating force of the opposition led by Britain.

There also appeared a flaw in the Nazi grand strategy, and this, too, worked towards an unfavourable condition for the Germans. During the autumn and winter of 1940, when Germany's air forces struck hardest, a point *Reichsmarschal* Herman Goering and other advocates of air power had consistently refused to believe, was resolved. Regardless of Germany's convictions to the contrary, no determined nation which was even moderately able to defend itself against convential air attacks could be defeated from the air. Britain, out-gunned, out-flown, and ceaselessly pounded by everything in the German air arsenal, was still down there, fighting back, while an exhausted and seriously decimated *Luftwaffe* had to desist.

Finally, during the autumn and winter of 1940, while Britain and her allies in disarray slowly recovered from disaster on the Continent and the debacle at Dunkirk, the first of an increasingly harmful series of sorties across the Channel against Germany's *Festung Europa* suggested that the *Blitzkrieg's* spectacular triumphs might possibly be vulnerable to the wearing-down, dogged variety of attrition, of which the British had always been masters.

Paris was dark, drab and cheerless, the winter of 1940, but elsewhere conditions were discernably and ominously changing. In the spirit of that change, the time for the *réseaux* network Armand and Mathilde Carré undertook to establish in Paris had arrived. The British, who were supposed to have surrendered, had not done so. The United States was becoming increasingly antagonistic toward Germany, and the blurred delineations of 1939 and early 1940 had hardened into distinctly recognisable areas of friend and foe. In France the general resistance of a conquered people was becoming increasingly hostile and widespread; but there were problems, the foremost of which were lack of arms, financing, and contact with Britain.

These factors were all favourable to Armand's undertaking. He and Mathilde Carré secured a very modest apartment in Paris, she, using her French Red Cross identification papers, Armand using his passport of the dead Frenchman, Armand Borni. They were exuberantly enthusiastic. Mathilde thrived on the excitement. When he laughed, so did she, when he became moody, her mood matched his. They went forth boldly to recruit. One of the first people they contacted was the uncle of a young man Mathilde had met at Vichy, Maitre Brault, a prominent French lawyer whose pre-war practice had been largely involved with English-speaking citizens, British and American.

Maitre Brault listened, was impressed by Armand's sincerity, and agreed to help. There were other contacts, many of them, but Maitre Brault, a man of substance and complete respectability, was a very important acquisition. He had contacts in London as well as in France. He journeyed to Bordeaux with Armand, introduced him to other Frenchmen whose positions would be invaluable, and gradually the initial phase of the network was forged. It was called *Interallié*, Inter-Allied.

Armand exploited his recruits, as he had done with Maitre Brault, to reach additional recruits. Every trustworthy French patriot knew other French patriots. At first, there was the basic requirement of living expenses to be satisfied. The more resisters he recruited, the more in the way of donations he got. But these were always meagre in Occupied France. Still, he and Mathilde got by, and their enthusiasm never waned. By the end of the winter they had more than a hundred recruits. Mathilde's father, who had won a decoration, the Legion of Honour, fighting the Germans in the First World War, was naturally proud of his daughter, although he and his wife saw very little of her at this time, even though they were all residents of Paris.

As the year 1940 drew to a close, Armand and Mathilde abandoned their flat on the rue de Faubourg St Jacques, and moved to a larger one at 14 rue de Colonel Moll. They now had a short-wave radio, and were beginning to receive intelligence reports from *Interallié* agents in a dozen major French cities.

Mathilde became Armand's courier, as well as his confidante. She also was a very successful recruiter and, in the course of her travels, again encountered her childhood friend, the former tank-corps captain, René Aubertin. He at once enlisted in the organization.

Armand, too, searched out old friends and allies. When his staff was completed, there were Poles as well as Frenchmen. Lieutenant Bernard Krutki, Armand's former aide, before the fall, was among them. So was a small, almost frail Polish aristocrat, another former officer, Lucien de Roquigny, who had at one time been associated with the department of French studies at the University of Warsaw. Another former Polish soldier was Stephane, who was used as one of Inter-Allied's couriers. He was especially valuable between Inter-Allied's Paris headquarters and the Polish-French underground at Marseilles.

There was even a seventeen-year-old Polish girl, Cipinka Lipsky, who worked closely with her father Wladimir Lipsky, the former commercial illustrator who coordinated espionage reports with Armand's growing file of maps, painstakingly maintaining current locations of every German installation, and troop dispersal in France.

A middle-aged Frenchman who had fought in World War

One, had been wounded in that earlier conflict against the Germans, Marc Marchal, code-named 'Uncle Marco', was recruited by René Aubertin, bearing out Armand's belief that one good recruit could find others as dependable. Marchal, 'Uncle Marco', was by trade a successful commercial chemist. He was also married, with four children. He was a handsome, genial, and fortunately, a very brave man.

There were many others: Mirielle Lejeune, whose husband was an inspector with the Paris police department. He was also recruited, and proved invaluable as a supplier of passes, top-level police information, and, eventually, warnings, when the Germans went spy-hunting. His code name was 'Boby Roland'.

Eventually, Armand's conviction that each recruit was a source for additional recruits proved almost awkwardly correct. Inter-Allied grew too fast, became vast and cumbersome, but such were conditions in France at the time that there was exactly the degree of cooperation which was required to make the Inter-Allied network function successfully.

Armand, who was very capable as a staff officer in a war-room full of maps during conventional warfare, was as capable now. Also, he had as aides, wiser, older, more experienced men, such as Maitre Brault and Marc Marchal – 'Uncle Marco'. And not only them; other Frenchmen of stature, serving in the wide-flung Inter-Allied cells, which soon covered more than half the country, worked as diligently and as selflessly as any of the enthusiastic younger people.

Some of the older people were occasionally 'horrified at Armand's and Mathilde's attitude of blithe imprudence. Once, Mathilde returned from a clandestine trip to boast of having cultivated a German officer, and of teasing him about the possibility of her being a French spy. Another time, when Maitre Brault visited the apartment at rue du Colonel Moll, Armand and his staff were studying maps on tables and on the walls, clearly marked with the dispositions of the enemy, without any sentry outside the door, acting as though Paris were not swarming with *Abwehr* and Gestapo agents. He said it made his hair stand on end, this complete lack of

precaution. He also said that although he admired Armand's
obvious organizational ability, his naïvety appalled him. At
this time Maitre Brault was deeply involved, as were they all;
he had got to know his fellow-conspirators very well. He said
Mathilde Carré's many-faceted personality increasingly
worried him.

There were others who should have been worried, but the
greying, handsome Lucien de Roguigny was not one of them.
He fell in love with Mathilde, a not unusual situation. When
Mathilde Carré went forth to recruit for Inter-Allied, in fact
when she went forth to do anything, she was completely
whole-hearted about it. As an extenuation of Armand,
whatever he desired, she used every resource she possessed to
obtain. Lucien de Roquigny was only one of many men who
either loved Mathilde, or who thought they did, but regardless
of that, Mathilde served only Inter-Allied and Roman
Czerniawski – Armand.

She was not alone in this dedication; they all worked
zealously at improving, at organizing, at improvising, for
Inter-Allied, but only Mathilde Carré's zealotry was
superficial; she served Inter-Allied because it, too, was an
extenuation of Armand.

Their network of 100 secret agents became more than two
hundred, with affiliated observers and informers scattered all
across France. From one radio transmitter, in Armand's flat,
Inter-Allied's transmitting and receiving stations, in Paris
alone, numbered four fully manned installations within only
weeks after the organization was initially founded; from a staff
of six or eight people, Armand's headquarters coterie grew
almost overnight to three times that many people.

Mail drops were established in cafés, in cloakrooms, in
private residences, even on trains. Information was delivered
to a specific drop, cached there, and was subsequently
retrieved by a secret agent whose specific obligation it was to
make prompt pick-ups in assigned sectors. A Pole named
Stanislas Lach, code-named 'Rapide', was especially valuable
at making pick-ups. He was also a daring and highly
successful courier who delivered secret documents to such
ports as Bordeaux and Marseilles, for transmittal to British

Intelligence, and any of those documents, if found on his person by the Germans, would have guaranteed his execution.

How the entire organization was so successfully put together and, more astonishingly, held together, by so many absolute amateurs, under the noses of Germany's vast Intelligence bureaus such as the *Abwehr*, the Gestapo, and, least admirable of all, the network of French informers hired by the Germans for no other purpose than to seek out such elements of the underground as Inter-Allied, was a genuine miracle.

The first Inter-Allied broadcast to London went out shortly after Christmas, 1940, but Inter-Allied's purpose and progress was already known to British Intelligence, earlier, by 16th November, 1940, and London was pleased at the extent and efficiency of the organization. Prior information from occupied France had come by way of Madrid, and it was usually so slow in arriving that it was already out-dated by the time it arrived. At least Royal Air Force bomber strikes against such objectives as troop-trains and German shipping could not be launched on information a week or two old.

Of course the answer to this condition was direct radio contact, and when that was established, in early 1941, conditions began to improve for the Allies, and to worsen for the Germans. But of course the Germans did not react with resignation, and as the early spring of the new year approached, German zeal in tracking down spies and saboteurs was expanded to include motorized radio-detection vans. These mobile units operated on a very simple principle of electronic detection. They cruised city streets in all the major metropolitan areas of France, and in conjunction with less sophisticated techniques for locating cells of *résistants*, such as torturing people until they named someone they knew who was associated with those groups, were very successful in literally eliminating hundreds of underground cells, and thousands of unfortunate French patriots.

By early 1941 the remarkably successful Inter-Allied organization had to face its first grave peril. The very situation it was working hardest to achieve, Allied havoc in Occupied France, which could, obviously, only be so highly successful because radios in France were guiding in the torpedoes and bombs, brought forth Germany's most skilled and deadly techniques of detection, as well as Germany's most indefatigable spy-hunters.

Meanwhile, the sturdy little green-eyed French woman wearing the black coat and red hat went assiduously on her assignments, still imbued with energetic enthusiasm, still motivated, in part, by the thrill of risk, and a personal idea of how clever she was; but mainly Lily Carré's motivation was Armand.

5

The Game Ceases To Be A Game

Each of Inter-Allied's individual cells, particularly those most distant from Paris, had its individual leader. Those directly subordinate to him had the responsibility of gathering information in assigned territories or neighbourhoods, as well as the duty of recruiting other dependable patriots who could also, in turn, gather information and recruit.

There was work for everyone. The press was closely scrutinized by former French newsmen. Anything worthwhile was gleaned and passed up to headquarters through the chain of organization. Farmers watched German truck convoys and troop-trains across the countryside, and reported. Artists sketched German installations, and furnished accurate drawings of the *Luftwaffe's* latest aircraft. Seamen reported German arrivals and departures from the ports and harbours. Savants interpreted, and deciphered, every scrap of written information. Street-sweepers reported which commandeered residences housed German officers, and which hotels and historic mansions were host to the German secret police and Intelligence units.

By the spring of 1941 France had become one vast espionage and sabotage network. The French took to this means of resistance with the ardour of a genuinely devious people. There was practically nothing the Germans could do without Armand's maps and confidential files – as well as his busy radios – reflecting it.

Mathilde Carré, in her capacity as courier, often returned from a round of 'drops' with an incredible wealth of critical information. Nor was she the only one. Inter-Allied's agents were everywhere.

Other *Résistance* organizations proliferated, and if they did not always co-operate among themselves, the Gaullists being antagonistic towards the pro-British, for example, and the Communists trusting neither, at least in their opposition to the Germans, they rarely betrayed one another. Furthermore, since Britain was the leader of Allied efforts at this time, if an air strike or a commando raid were desired, the Intelligence concerning such endeavours had to be approved by London, if it was approved at all, consequently, whether the underground network was pro-British or anti-British, there was only one major power it could contact for action.

Wars have always made strange bedfellows, but if the objective has been to *win*, then of course political, ideological, or other kinds of disparities have had to be subjugated. They were, by and large, in France in 1941. Whoever it was a particular *réseau* disliked, it was a fact that its members disliked the Germans more.

Inter-Allied encountered other networks, but its early pre-eminence in the field gave it a healthy head-start, and when the British were contacted for aid and support, this being almost immediately forthcoming, Inter-Allied's pre-eminence was confirmed.

Armand's cooperation with the British resolved two pressing difficulties. One was the matter of a mutual code, the other was the matter of funds. It took a heavy burden off his shoulders, and as his spirits soared, so also did the spirits of Mathilde Carré, who now more than ever became his close confidant and general aide.

Radio transmission from the rue du Colonel Moll was begun immediately. The vast fund of information to be transmitted amounted to a great windfall for the British. It was directed to Room 55A of the War Office, where, within a short space of time, anything arriving from France signed Armand or the Cat, received priority rating and immediate consideration. Inter-Allied agents from Cherbourg, Boulogne, Brest, Calais, from Hendaye, Biarritz and Bordeaux, fed a steady stream of information to Paris, which was transmitted to London, and consequently, as it occasionally happened, German ships were sunk in place, and laden troop-trains were bombed in transit.

Mathilde spent more and more time co-ordinating information, and helping to code and transmit it. Her signature on communications – the Cat – continually turned up in London. She and Armand encapsuled stolen and copied German directives and orders, as well as the latest strategic maps, and sent them to London, along with very accurate art-work depicting German air fields, camps, even French factories manufacturing war-wares for Hitler's *Stahlhelm*.

Marc Marchal – Uncle Marco – helped Mathilde obtain a restricted, complete set of timetables for German military trains, a priceless aid for Royal Air Force bombings, as well as for demolition experts among France's increasingly bold saboteurs.

Colonel Zarembski's 'Tudor' organization and Armand's Inter-Allied network blanketed the whole of France between them. It became almost an impossibility for the Germans to do anything at all without one organization or the other monitoring their activities, which, by itself would have created little enough difficulty, since neither organization, prior to their association with London, could mount more than nuisance raids in the way of opposition. But once Tudor and Inter-Allied began supplying the British with entirely reliable Intelligence, conditions changed fast, drastically, and, for France's secret agents and their organizations, dangerously.

The Germans had suffered from sabotage of one kind and another beginning shortly after the French surrender, but usually in isolated, not very crippling, instances. Nevertheless, their reaction, even in those early days, had been swift and remorseless. Therefore, when, by the summer of 1941, it became quite obvious that what was now occurring was something devastatingly different, German fury increased correspondingly to the extent of the new opposition.

German airfields were located and bombed, German railroad concentrations were caught before dispersal was possible; serious blows were struck, in places, and at the exact times, when maximum harm was possible. There clearly had to be several skilled and efficient *Résistance* organisations at work. German controls were increased. Motorized units descended without warning on business establishments and

residences, burst in and made thorough searches. Inevitably a
few people were shot, being unable to dispose of incriminating
scraps of information in time, but the general result of all this
did not initially affect French *Résistance* very much.

The threat to French *résistants* was very real, and it would
become increasingly so as German anger and detection
techniques resulted in strengthened *Abwehr* and Gestapo
efficiency, but for a while the successful people of Inter-Allied
conducted their clandestine affairs without excessive worry.

In one instance out of many, Marc Marchal demonstrated
that a commercial chemist could be a useful scholar. As a
result of British bombings of their airfields, the Germans
undertook construction of underground hangars. Marchal
created a chemical solution which, when mixed with cement,
prevented bonding. This concoction was surreptitiously
introduced into the mortar of German underground hangars
with, for the French, very gratifying results.

This, and other acts of sabotage could not always be kept
from the French public, and each act seemed to inspire
additional acts of sabotage. Much of the havoc was poorly
conceived and executed, and many amateurs were shot on the
spot, but the important thing was that French retaliation was
being encouraged, and the Germans were being compelled to
take note of a very serious, widespread, and increasingly
damaging, expansion of underground opposition in France, in
the late spring and early summer of 1941, at a time when the
High Command was required to implement *Der Führer*'s War
Directive Number twenty one, which said in part that "the
German Armed Forces must be prepared, even before the
conclusion of the war against England, to crush Soviet
Russia".

The result of these coinciding events was that when Nazi
Germany's 'Operation Barbarossa', the invasion of the Soviet
Union, was begun on 22nd June 1941, German occupation
troops could not safely be pared below a certain level in
France, in the face of the mounting underground opposition,
which was now obviously very skilled, and which was just as
obviously functioning in consort with London.

The obvious solution was of course to concentrate on

destruction of *Résistance* networks and for this the Germans had the largest, if not the best, Intelligence and counter-Intelligence establishments in the world, at that time.

While stiffening, and reinforced, German opposition to underground activity in France was becoming more efficient, the co-operation, however, between Inter-Allied and London was also achieving an apex. 'Rapide' and scores of other Inter-Allied agents, including the small French woman in the black coat and pert red hat, circulated almost effortlessly, gathering information for evaluation and subsequent transmittal to London, with the result that air strikes and commando raids considerably increased.

Among the information sent to British Intelligence was the name of local German commandants, markings on aircraft, sketches of aircraft, numbers and locations of both aircraft and motorized army elements, locations of factories engaged in producing material for the Germans, together with sketches, or, if possible, photographs of camouflage, locations of German camps and stations, information about aircraft and coastal defences, insignia on cars, uniforms, trucks, trains, and London also asked for, and was sent, anything which could be utilized in propaganda broadcasts.

The flow of intelligence became steadily greater and more sophisticated. Occasional failures were inevitable, as when an attempt to secure a sample of a virus culture being developed under German supervision in a Vincennes laboratory for use as a weapon of germ warfare, was thwarted by a zealous guard, and again, when German ingenuity caused confusion through the use of false insignia, but in comparison to the amount of reliable information transmitted to London the failures were negligible.

Armand's zeal was tireless. As German counter-Intelligence became more of a threat, Armand's directives to Inter-Allied's cells repeatedly stressed tighter secrecy and greater precautions. On the other hand, Mathilde Carré developed a harrowing routine of deliberately cultivating German officers along the boulevards and in the cafés, and artfully extracting what information she could from them. The danger inherent in this game did not entirely derive from the Germans. Many

Frenchmen, seeing a French woman in the company of a German, and believing her to be a collaborator, were perfectly willing patiently to await an opportunity, then administer a beating. These occurrences were commonplace.

Mathilde, however, was fortunate. She was many times glared at, but never attacked. However, she developed an over-confidence that would have frightened Maitre Brault half to death, if he had known about it. Her acting, though, to give full credit, brought in valued information. Her code name on messages to London – dash dot-dash dot-dot dash-dash – signified valuable and reliable information.

As a result of Royal Air Force strikes at the seaport of Brest, at the westernmost tip of France, which were the result of Inter-Allied intelligence supplied London, Mathilde journeyed there from Paris, at Armand's request, to evaluate the damage. It was known that Brest, nearly opposite Plymouth, on England's south coast across the Channel, was a bulwark of pro-British sentiment, despite the ruin caused by Royal Air Force bombings. It was one of the first major French cities to fall, when German armour, under General Heinz Guderian, captured it on 17th September, 1939. It was, at the time of Mathilde's arrival, in the process of being blockaded from the sea by German warships, who were in turn, under British naval surveillance. Germans were in absolute control, and their domination was harsh. It also happened that the port of Brest was a hotbed of intrigue.

Mathilde chose as her disguise the appearance of an English woman. In this capacity she felt sure of gaining the confidence of the local residents. She visited the ruined harbour facilities, and the shops, which were also largely demolished. In one store she evinced interest in the willingness of the people to keep their stores open, and in the course of a conversation with a clerk, using English-accented French, Mathilde was over-heard by a man in civilian attire who, when she departed, followed her.

At day's end, having seen as much as was necessary in order to give Armand a complete report, Mathilde boarded a train for Paris, and the young man in civilian attire boarded the same train.

Mathilde did not realize she was being followed until the train reached Paris. If she had not discovered it by then, a very real disaster could have ensued for the entire Inter-Allied organization, but even so, it was more the result of her shadow's lack of patience than Mathilde's cleverness that prevented this. After they left the train the young man's obvious interest culminated when he approached and asked a simple question in French. Mathilde answered, in her normal language, and the young man then said, "But you have no accent, Madame." Mathilde's retort was to the effect that Parisians did not have an accent, and who was he, anyway?

He was an agent of the Gestapo, he told her, and had followed her from Brest, where he thought he had detected an English accent. He then asked what her business had been in Brest.

For Mathilde Carré, the moment was tailored to her qualifications. She smiled at the Gestapo agent. They sought a café and there she said that she had heard so much of the ruin occasioned by Royal Air Force bombings, that out of womanly curiosity, she had decided to visit Brest to see for herself if the damage was really as extensive as she had heard. And since everyone knew the residents of Brest were pro-British, she had decided to pretend to be British, which obviously she was not, in order to encourage the people she met to converse with a stranger. It was all a joke, actually. She certainly had not anticipated that this small ruse would come to the attention of the German authorities.

Mathilde was very fortunate. Her new acquaintance was willing to allow the matter to end there, in exchange for her companionship. The affair was eventually resolved, they parted, and Mathilde went on to give her report to Armand. She could have been followed again, and a different Gestapo agent certainly would have followed her. This agent did not. Subsequently, Armand reported to London how successful the strike at Brest had been. Subsequently, too, paralleling events brought danger closer. Detection vans of the *Funkpeildienst* became commonplace sights on the boulevards of Paris. They appeared also in other major French cities, as well as in the countryside. Inside each van a German technician manned radio monitoring devices. As the tempo of transmission to London increased, so also did the hazards increase for the operators of clandestine transmission facilities. Apprehension followed, naturally, until the point was reached where it was not safe to transmit at all, not even at night, when most contacts were made, and not for more than a few days at a time in the same locations. Informants watched the vans closely. A new kind of underground surveillance was inaugurated. When the vans were noticed to be slowly patrolling an area, warnings were passed in every adjoining neighbourhood.

Mathilde and Armand were eventually warned that the detection vans had been seen in the area of their rue du Colonel Moll headquarters. By this time their value to British Intelligence had also increased the peril in other ways. Air-drops of arms, funds, and radio equipment, nearly all of which required hiding before it could be dispersed, had created problems. There was also the matter of air-dropped Allied secret agents, and radio operators. The entire situation was changing. The initial era, when espionage had been largely a game to Armand and Mathilde, had ended. From the summer of 1941 onward, there would be fewer and fewer moments of gaiety. Ultimately, too, the danger of Inter-Allied being penetrated by either agents of German counter-intelligence, or by French informers (called V-men, *Vertrauensmänner*, trusted informers) became more of a threat. The Gestapo, *Abwehr*, and the French cliques who were in the employment of one or the other, sharpened their techniques of detection to a very high degree, and although, in general, German counter-Intelligence was never to achieve the sophistication and expertise of the British, there were particular Germans who would rival their foes, especially in Occupied France.

Eventually, Mathilde and Armand, in conference with the staff and major supporters of Inter-Allied, decided that some changes had to be made. A number of cells were directed to change locations, not only of their radio posts, but of their meeting places as well.

It was this eleventh-hour decision that undoubtedly prevented the Germans from apprehending anyone from

Inter-Allied at this time. They knew, of course, that such an organization existed, and they had tried very hard to catch at least one member of it. Some of the people they apprehended confirmed, under interrogation, that Inter-Allied existed, but the web of subterfuge, aliases, disguises, code-names instead of actual names, and now, the changing of locations, prevented a German success.

In late 1941, as a result of *Funkpeildienst* interest in their neighbourhood, Mathilde and Armand decided to move. Mathilde searched for a new location, and eventually found a small, quite old, multi-storeyed house, 8 Villa Léandre, on Avenue Junot, in an elevated section of Montmartre.

This occurred in October. The previous month British Intelligence – often referred to collectively as either 'SIS' or 'British Secret Service', designations covering all aspects of British Intelligence – asked Armand to come to London for a series of talks. This request was handled through Special Operation Executive – SOE – French Section, which was in 1941 headed by Colonel Maurice J. Buckmaster.

October turned out to be a busy, and in some ways, a rewarding month for Inter-Allied. The move to the quaint, red-roofed house in Montmartre was made, then, on the first day of October, Colonel Buckmaster's French Section of SOE sent a light aircraft, a Lysander, to a field near Estrees – St Denis, where Armand was picked up and flown to London.

6
One Year Of Success

Armand spent nine days in London. He met with British Intelligence officers at their headquarters at St James, and in Bayswater. He received a commendation by the War Office, met with high-ranking officials of the Polish government in exile, and General Sikorski awarded him the Order of Virtuti Militari, his country's highest decoration for gallantry.

From these meetings Armand derived valuable information concerning the functions of British Intelligence as it was related to his Inter-Allied network. He was eventually returned to France, in the vicinity of Tours, 9th October, and was subsequently able to inform his staff, including Mathilde Carré, that he had been assured at SOE's Baker Street headquarters that British secret agents would shortly be air-dropped to aid Inter-Allied in its major objectives of espionage and sabotage.

This month, too, the removal to the little red-roofed house on the Avenue Junot was accomplished. The owner of the house, an aged widow of a French Colonel of the First World War, Madame Blavette, was captivated by Mathilde, who brought a little sunshine into the aged woman's otherwise troubled and anxious existence. To account for the nocturnal comings and goings, Mathilde explained, between women, that her "cousin" Armand, who shared the upstairs quarters with her, was engaged in a little harmless black marketing. Madame assured the stocky, green-eyed Mathilde, that nothing would be said; in those days, alas, everyone must, at one time or another, go to the black market; France had fallen upon terrible times.

Finally, this fateful month, Armand made still another move, and this was to be the most disastrous one of his career. He, who had enjoined secrecy and caution so strongly on others, as the Germans heightened their counter-intelligence endeavours, perhaps as a result of the commendations received in London, and believing himself superior in all ways to the enemy, brought the soft and ardent widow of Armand Borni to Montmartre.

He had not told Mathilde of Renée Borni, the uncomplicated, physically appealing, not-very-bright widow of Lunéville. There can be no doubt that these two women could never have been compatible under any circumstances. Renée was as voluptuous, as sexually attractive and compliant, as Mathilde, but in a completely different way. Mathilde had a need for Armand, expressed sexually of course, in a most demanding and exhausting way, but her need went much deeper, it was also the hunger of a leeching, unformed character. It was food for her soul, and she had never been capable of surviving without it for any length of time. She was only a complete woman when she could nourish her emptiness from someone else, and, being a woman with tremendous physical vitality, her requirement was for men of strong impulses.

Renée Borni, on the other hand, was a domesticated woman. Her need was also for a man, but the demand was not voracious; it was instead, passive and soft, yielding and loving. Renée, under other circumstances, would undoubtedly have re-married, lived and died in a tidy house, with children, and a husband capable of being satisfied with good meals and a devoted woman. Wartime France offered these opportunities, but not for Renée, once the Polish soldier appeared. In fact, for Renée Borni, France would never offer them, although it is reasonable to believe she thought it had, when Armand sent for her, and she duly arrived in Paris with no knowledge that Mathilde Carré existed.

Armand, who had created a successful and far-flung espionage and sabotage organization, who could understand and manipulate people so well, had succumbed to the most fatal shortcoming of most men – his own vanity. He had, by this time, been living with Lily Carré about a year. He certainly knew her temperament, whether he understood why she was as she was, or not. He knew she was capable of fierce jealousies as well as of equally fierce attachments. He, who had consistently warned others of imprudence, now introduced a former mistress to his current one.

Even docile Renée was capable of hatred. From the moment they met, Renée and Mathilde fiercely and savagely despised one another. They became more than rivals for the affection of Armand, they became personal enemies on other grounds as well, but it was all based on their jealousy of one another. Mathilde could not face the possible loss of her love, her other self. Renée could not accept the idea of sharing the man she had loved in Lunéville, and about whom she had been fantasizing ever since.

To Mathilde, Renée was stupid – a country woman. To Renée, Mathilde was evil. To Armand, and his vanity, which had been so immensely flattered in London, the acquisition of Renée offered variety. He taught her how to code and de-code messages. Her code name became 'Violette'. Among the Inter-Allied staff she became in time, to be recognized as an adequately competent person, of no particular ability, at least of no outstanding ability, but as the work-load increased, she carried her part of it well enough.

Mathilde moved out of the house on Avenue Junot. She still faithfully performed her duties. The little red hat and black coat were as familiar as ever as she made her rounds, gathering information from the 'drops', attending meetings, arranging secret rendezvous. She moved into a room on the Rue Cortot, in Montmartre, and for a time was able to sustain herself by a frenzied devotion to her work.

Armand, too, concentrated on work. Inter-Allied's messages to London consistently exposed the Germans to Allied attacks, and the Germans reacted with even greater efforts. On 16th November 1941, Armand called together his closest associates of Inter-Allied for a quiet anniversary celebration. In a year, the organization had grown from two people, Armand and Mathilde, to the most productive and resourceful of the French underground espionage networks. It had received compliments from London, usually *via* the BBC's Continental broadcasts. Its leader had been the recipient of a gallantry award. The others did not know it, but Armand, with an eye on the future, when the Germans would be defeated and the works of those who had aided that defeat would be in demand, had been keeping a diary, a journal of everything that had been done, complete with dates, places, and real names. It was entitled *One Year of Inter-Allied*.

Part of Armand's surprise for those, including Mathilde, who were invited to the Avenue Junot headquarters for the anniversary party, was a message of congratulation from London, beamed to Paris by the BBC, every broadcast of which was monitored by German Intelligence.

Mathilde was escorted to the party by René Aubertin. They went first to a small café for dinner. Mirielle Lejeune accompanied them to the café, but not to the party. They took Mirielle home, then proceeded without haste to the party. There were several recent untoward events to be discussed. For one thing a couple named Hugentobler who served the Paris network, had reported a recent interrogation at their home on the Avenue Lamarck by a Gestapo team, who had also searched their residence, used frequently by the organization. How the Germans had happened to visit these people, a man and wife from Alsace, was both puzzling and disturbing.

More disturbing was the recent arrest in Cherbourg of an Inter-Allied agent, the first apprehension, thus far, of someone directly connected with the organization.

What René and Mathilde feared was that the arrest in Cherbourg would put everyone connected with Inter-Allied in jeopardy, for, even assuming the captured agent only knew his immediate superiors, German methods of interrogation were very thorough; one agent led to another, and so on, to the top.

The party was not a success. Everyone knew of the Cherbourg affair, and most had heard of the Gestapo's visit to the Hugentoblers. Also, Renée Borni – 'Violette' – acted for Armand in the capacity of hostess, a role previously undertaken by Mathilde. It made the guests uncomfortable. By this time everyone connected with Inter-Allied headquarters was aware that Renée, not Mathilde, now shared Armand's interludes of relaxation. Nothing was said at the party, but the atmosphere was uncomfortable. The guests were roughly divided between French and Poles. At least one of the men, Claude Jouffret, was already prepared to sacrifice the others at the first scent of danger.

There was no gaiety. Champagne was served, and in all there were somewhat fewer than a dozen of Inter-Allied's leadership present. Armand was a good host, if not an exuberant one, and once, when Renée baited Mathilde by mentioning a recent present she had received from Armand, the hurt and angered Mathilde reacted with verbal abuse, and Armand had diplomatically to separate the women.

The guests were willing to leave early, but Armand's surprise was not due to be broadcast until later, so they waited. Eventually the BBC came over the radio, first with the news bulletins, then, finally with the personal items, one of which was a congratulatory commendation upon the "... *anniversaire à la famille réunie á Paris*." It was repeated twice. Everyone showed some evidence of appreciation. Armand directed that Inter-Allied respond. The proper signal of transmission was sent forth, then the message: "*Vive la liberté*", and of course all of this was monitored by the Germans.

The party ended before midnight. René escorted Mathilde to her room on the Avenue Cortot, the others went to their separate residences, leaving Armand and Renée at the house on the Avenue Junot. Armand's party, which had not been a very great success, presaged bitter changes for Inter-Allied. The anniversary of one successful year was anything but a guarantee of future success.

At this time one of SOE's most valued agents, Captain Pierre de Vomécourt, a former officer of the French Chasseur battalions, educated in England, scion of an aristocratic French family, and the first SOE agent of F-Section to return to France after the fall, contacted an old pre-war acquaintance, Maitre Brault, seeking to be put in touch with Inter-Allied, after the *réseau* he had been air-dropped to organize, called 'Autogiro', had been penetrated by the Germans and its few survivors scattered.

Maitre Brault, who could vouch for de Vomécourt, explained about Armand, Mathilde, and Inter-Allied's

organization, and agreed to arrange for de Vomécourt to meet
Mathilde.

Before this meeting could take place, others who were also
anxious to meet the French woman whose red hat and black
coat were well-known to the underground, were already at
work to effect a meeting. They were the Germans who had for
so long been trying to penetrate Inter-Allied. Their success
was a result of that apprehension at Cherbourg, Mathilde and
René Aubertin had discussed after dinner the evening of
Armand's party, and in itself, it was perhaps the most
ignominious of all harbingers of disaster. Its principal actor
was a dissolute French dockworker, who, in the company of a
young German corporal, with whom the dockworker had
struck up a drinking companionship, sat in a waterfront café
in Cherbourg one evening, and made a maudlin confession. A
woman he knew, a certain Charlotte Bouffet had asked the
dockworker to do her a small favour – supply her with a
written and detailed list of *Luftwaffe* aircraft and supplies at
the depot where the dockworker was presently employed.

He had supplied the woman with some information,
nothing important, but it was troubling the dockworker's
conscience; he did not want to end up in any trouble, and in
any case he thought the woman might belong to one of those
Résistance cells, something the dockworker preferred to have
nothing to do with. The war would end, some day, in its own
good time, and meanwhile a man did what he must in order to
survive, and obviously, the surest way to do that was to avoid
involvement of any kind.

The German corporal relayed all this to his superiors of the
Luftwaffe, who were not concerned with espionage. Their
responsibility ended when a report was duly filed with the
Geheime Feldpolizei of Cherbourg. From there it was sent, by
Schar-Führer (Sergeant) Hugo Bleicher to *Abwehr III* – Third
Section of Military Intelligence – whose responsibility was the
entire area of north-western France, and whose function was
the hunting-down and apprehending of all enemy agents,
spies, saboteurs, and informers for the Allied forces.

Abwehr III had its headquarters in a palatial villa at
Maisons Lafitte, the former residence of a French-Jewish

actor named Harry Baur, who did not survive the war. Known as *Abwehr* St Germain, the personnel of the Maisons Lafitte villa had received their share of upbraiding over the successes of the, up-to-now-unknown, *Résistance* group known in London as Inter-Allied. The *Luftwaffe* report of a possible female spy in Cherbourg caused no great stir, but it was to be investigated, of course. No one had any idea where it would lead.

Sturmbann-Führer Eshig, commandant of *Abwehr* St Germain, sent *Obersturm-Führer* (Captain) Erich Borchers to Cherbourg to locate and interrogate Madame Bouffet. Captain Borchers, a pre-war Rhineland newspaper journalist, did not possess a good command of French. Neither was he familiar with the vast port-complex of Cherbourg. Upon arriving there he went first to the *Luftwaffe* security command for help, and when no one there was able to lend assistance, Captain Borchers went to the same office of the army's field police, the *Geheime Feldpolizei*, which had relayed the information to *Abwehr III* from the *Luftwaffe*, in the first place.

The man Captain Borchers met was the same sergeant, Hugo Bleicher, who had inaugurated the forwarding action of the *Luftwaffe* report. Erich Borchers had come full circle.

The man Bleicher deserves more than passing mention. His part in what followed, despite his NCO status, overshadowed the role of Captain Borchers, and all other Germans of the Occupation security forces.

At the time he and Captain Borchers met at the Cherbourg field police station, Sergeant Bleicher was nothing more than a non-commissioned officer of the German military police. Neither he nor his field police unit had anything whatever to do with espionage or counter-intelligence, which were *Abwehr* responsibilities.

Hugo Ernst Bleicher's meeting with Erich Borchers was to launch him into the annals of the Second World War counter-Intelligence, and although he never achieved a rank above sergeant, Bleicher became one of the most successful and outstanding German counter-Intelligence officers of the war. Subsequently, he achieved a number of notable successes. After his lurid encounter with Inter-Allied, and Mathilde

Carré, he went on to other equally spectacular assignments, and in 1943, at St Jorioz, he apprehended Peter Churchill, and his companion Odette Sansom (subsequently Mrs Churchill) who were among the top SOE agents of the war.

Hugo Bleicher was not a young man at the outbreak of the Second World War. At the age of seventeen he had served in the German army during the First World War, had been wounded and captured at Verdun. Poor eye-sight bothered him all his life. He had been educated at Ravensburg University, came from a solid middle-class family, and had an excellent command of languages, including French. He was a talented pianist, had been employed between wars as a bank clerk, an interpreter, German export official in Morocco, and in 1929 married Lucie Mueller, with whom he established a home in the suburb of Poppensbüttel. He and Frau Bleicher had one son.

Bleicher became a member of the German National Socialist Party when Adolf Hitler rose to power. At the outbreak of war he joined the Field Security Police, was stationed for a while in Holland, then was transferred to France. He was fluent in both French and English. Also, Hugo Bleicher was not the stereotype German security official. He did not employ Gestapo methods. Bleicher was a good manhunter who never resorted to torture. He believed that a counter-Intelligence officer should be able to match wits successfully with his enemies, and not have to torture information out of them. For a German soldier, he was unusually urbane. But he was neither weak nor gullible, and when he arrived in Cherbourg in early 1941, from St Lo in Normandy, he was a conqueror, as were all Germans in Occupied Europe at that time.

The war was not a series of hardships for Sergeant Bleicher, as it was for many German soldiers. He saw no combat, was comfortably housed throughout, and while stationed at St Lo, cultivated a handsome French woman, Suzanne Laurent, who remained his mistress until the Nazi collapse in 1945, at which time he was forty-six years of age.

After the war Hugo Bleicher was captured in Holland by Canadian troops, on 15th June 1945, and taken to London,

where he was incarcerated and interrogated by officers of
SOE. He was not charged, and was sent next to Paris where
he was jailed as a suspected war criminal, but, as a result of
favourable testimony by his former enemies, Bleicher was
released in late 1946, and sent to Germany. He returned twice
to France after the war, once as a witness in war-crimes trials
of French collaborationists, and the last time, with Frau
Bleicher, as guests of the SOE agents, Peter and Odette
Churchill, whom he had captured in 1943.

Bleicher was not in appearance the Hollywood prototype of
either a spy-catcher or a stalwart *Stahlhelm*. In height and
build he was average, his hair was thin, straight, and greying,
his mouth was wide, poorly shaped and had a perpetual droop
at the corners. His weak eyes behind thick lenses were
practically colourless, their gaze unsmiling, direct, and
shrewd.

His general appearance was anything but romantic,
handsome, or spectacular, and that no doubt was against him
in the heyday of stalwart handsome Nazis such as Otto
Skorzeny and Baldur von Shirach. But once his real talent was
allowed to surface, this unprepossessing sergeant of the
military police became the ace of the *Abwehr*.

7

"That's Her, That's The Cat!"

The German military police were strictly functional at the *Feldwebel* level. They at no time had the influence or prestige of The *Sicherheitdienst* (SD), the elite *Schutzstaffeln* (SS), or either the Gestapo or the *Abwehr*. Captain Borchers was an *Abwehr* officer. When he appeared at the Cherbourg police station in need of someone who could speak French, and who knew the Cherbourg area, it was the responsibility of the lowly military police to aid him. The duty-sergeant that day was unprepossessing Hugo Bleicher, who volunteered to assist Borchers in locating the French woman alleged to have solicited restricted information.

Borchers and Bleicher went first to the *Luftwaffe* depot where the aged French dockworker was employed. They arrested him, and in quaking dread he answered their questions.

It turned out that, actually, he knew a little more than he had told his friend, the German corporal. As he had said, he knew the woman who had asked him to help her get information, Charlotte Bouffet, but he also knew more than her name, and that she was a resident of his neighbourhood. He knew, for example, that Charlotte Bouffet met a Frenchman called 'Kiki' once a month at the railroad depot, and received from this man money for the information she had collected for him. He also knew that 'Kiki' was the head of a *réseau* which covered six departments of northern France, including all of Brittany and the western sectors of Normandy, which was quite a bit for a man who had only told his drinking companion, the German corporal, that he thought Madame Bouffet might be engaged in espionage.

It was the second week of October; 'Kiki' only arrived in

Cherbourg, (from Paris or Lisieux, where Section D of Inter-Allied had a regional headquarters) on the first of each month. But Captain Borchers and Sergeant Bleicher did not have to waste time for two weeks. They located Charlotte Bouffet at her flat, arrested her – she was terror-stricken when uniformed Germans appeared at her door – and ransacked the apartment. Here, they got their first windfall: Madame Bouffet had a horde of notes given her for delivery to 'Kiki' by local informers. Borchers and Bleicher had all the evidence of espionage they needed. But there was more. Madame Bouffet kept a list of her sub-agents, by name. They included policemen, dockworkers, neighbours, labourers, and even postmen. Twenty people in all.

For the two weeks Borchers and Bleicher had to wait until 'Kiki' arrived, they were kept busy apprehending everyone on the Bouffet list. But no one knew, except in a vague way, where the secret information they gathered for Charlotte Bouffet, went. They only knew that 'Kiki' arrived, took the information, left funds to reimburse them, and departed. Even Charlotte Bouffet knew only that 'Kiki' was French, and that his code name was Paul. She of course knew him by sight, but when the first day of November arrived, the Germans did not use her to trap Paul, they took the dockworker with them to the depot, and stationed him where he could see every debarking passenger.

Paul was not among the people who got off the train. For Borchers and Bleicher the disappointment was great. They had not overlooked the possibility that someone might have reached Paul with a warning that Bouffet's *réseau* had been penetrated.

On 2nd November they again took the dockworker to the depot. Paul did not arrive on that day either. The anxiety of Borchers and Bleicher was increasing. On 3rd November they, and their alcoholic, and involuntary collaborator, went again to the depot. This time the dockworker, positioned at the exit gate for passengers, waited until a youthful Frenchman walked up, then pointed. At once the Germans moved forward and arrested their man. Both he and the dockworker were taken to the fortress in Cherbourg, where the hapless dockworker was returned to his cell, and Paul – or 'Kiki' – was taken to an interrogation chamber.

It was this apprehension of Paul, whose real name was Raoul Kiffer, that had so worried Mathilde Carré and René Aubertin, the evening of Armand's anniversary party. But neither Mathilde or René realised how genuine and imminent their peril was.

Paul – Raoul Kiffer – had in his pockets, at the time of his arrest, notes on German military installations in the Calvados, through which he had recently journeyed on his way to Cherbourg. These notes had been given him in the same way Charlotte Bouffet delivered her information to him. They presented Borchers and Sergeant Bleicher with additional information concerning what was now beginning to appear as an extensive espionage network.

Kiffer, whose genuine nick-name was Kiki, told his captors nothing, at first, beyond his name, and that he was a former non-commissioned officer of the French Air Force. But Sergeant Bleicher demonstrated the unique interrogation ability which in later years was to make him foremost among German counter-intelligence personnel. He showed Kiffer the list of sub-agents he had acquired from the Bouffet apartment. He explained that all those people were now in German custody. He told Kiffer that before the round-up of agents in both Cherbourg and the Calvados was completed, he would have all the information he required, in any case, and Kiffer's only hope of eluding the Gestapo, whose methods were of course, painfully notorious, would be to help Bleicher, who could then help Kiffer.

It was a persuasive argument. Just to mention the name of the Gestapo inspired terror.

Kiffer told the Germans that he was only a courier, a person who made the rounds gathering information. Bleicher was agreeable to this, but even a courier knew the man to whom the gathered intelligence was presented. Kiffer sweated. Finally, he told how he had been recruited in Paris to work for the organization, and Hugo Bleicher picked the key word from this statement – Paris.

Kiffer maintained that he did not know the name of the

organization's chief, and did not know where headquarters were. Bleicher was sympathetic. Still, if Kiffer did not know these things, he certainly had to know where he deposited the information he gathered. Kiffer got in deeper each time he answered a question. He deposited his intelligence information, he said, at a 'dropsite' at the Montparnasse café called La Palette, a well-known haunt in pre-war times of writers and painters. Again, the key word was Paris.

Captain Borchers and Sergeant Bleicher entrained from Cherbourg for Paris, with their prisoner. Bleicher was a pleasant travelling companion. He was never loud or threatening; he was considerate of the prisoner's well-being. After reaching Paris, Borchers, the *Abwehr* officer, took them both to St Germain-en-Laye. Here, Raoul Kiffer's resolve cracked a little more. Actually, by late 1941, it did not take much more than a realization that one was balancing on the edge of being handed over to the Gestapo to encourage co-operation. Not that many French people chose this course, but Raoul Kiffer did.

When Bleicher convinced him that there was no possible way for Bleicher or anyone else to save him from the Gestapo's torture chambers, unless he co-operated, and also very convincingly told Kiffer that he had been betrayed, Kiffer yielded.

Once converted to the status of traitor, what the Germans called a *Vertrauensmann*, or V-man, meaning an informer whose information could be relied upon, Raoul Kiffer went the full course. It was certainly not admirable, and after the war Kiffer was tried in a French court for treason and sentenced to prison, but at the time he was a prisoner of *Abwehr* St Germain, he really only had two choices, and he took the least painful one. His decision so delighted the *Abwehr* officials, that they requested that Hugo Bleicher be transferred to their department from the military police, which was accomplished in due course. Henceforth it was *Schar-Führer* Hugo Bleicher of the *Abwehr*.

When Bleicher was satisfied that Kiffer would sincerely co-operate he had the Frenchman released from custody to deliver a bogus bit of information to the cloakroom attendant at the Café La Palette. Kiffer was of course followed by *Abwehr* officers during this interlude. Bleicher then instituted a round-the-clock surveillance on the café cloakroom.

Several days passed before one of Armand's couriers arrived. It was not, although it could easily have been, Mathilde Carré. The agent Bleicher arrested as he picked up the envelope in the cloakroom, whose code-name was Christian, was Armand's war-time aide and long-time friend, Bernard Krutki. He was taken at once to the local *Abwehr* prison, where Bleicher almost met his match.

Krutki would reveal nothing. When Bleicher used the technique which had dissolved Kiffer's resolve, mentioning that Krutki would have to be delivered to the Gestapo unless he co-operated, the Pole would not budge. Bleicher spent hours with Krutki trying persecution, trying congeniality, even valid logic. The Pole remained unmoved and adamant. Bleicher pretended to give up, and allowed his other 'prisoner' Raoul Kiffer to visit Krutki's cell. With no way of knowing that Kiffer was now a double agent, was supposedly still loyal to Inter-Allied while actually serving the Germans, Bernard Krutki conversed guardedly but openly, and during the course of their conversation mentioned the address on Avenue Junot, 8 Villa Léandre, where Armand had his headquarters. That was all Bleicher had been waiting to hear.

This inadvertent betrayal by the courageous Pole occurred the very evening when Mathilde and René Aubertin were anxiously discussing the arrest of the agent in Cherbourg, while on their way to Armand's anniversary party, on 16th November 1941, which was a Sunday.

If Bleicher had gone at once to the red-roofed house on Avenue Junot, he would have bagged the entire top leadership of Inter-Allied. But Hugo Bleicher was a methodical man of awesome patience and orderly perseverence. All day Monday, 17th November, Sergeant Bleicher organized his surprise party. Several squads of German police were called up, trucks to transport them, and their weapons, were requisitioned, Madame Blavette's house and neighbourhood were put under surveillance, and when all was in readiness, Captain Borchers and Sergeant Bleicher established the time for their strike to be shortly before dawn on Tuesday 18th November.

In the pre-daylight gloom, finally, at three o'clock in the morning, the army trucks arrived on the Avenue Junot, the house was quickly surrounded, and when Sergeant Bleicher rapped on Madame Blavette's street door, and the aged widow opened it, she was shouldered aside by Germans who quickly ran up the stairs.

Armand was standing in the centre of his parlour, which was also Inter-Allied's map and strategy chamber, clad in pyjamas, when armed Germans burst through the door. He was taken completely by surprise. In the adjoining bedroom, awakened from a sound slumber, was Renée Borni. It was subsequently claimed that a third person, a man, had been in the apartment that very morning, and being alarmed at the sound of many booted feet charging up the stairs, had escaped out of a window across the rooftops to safety. Perhaps – in any event it did not matter.

Confronted by Captain Borchers and Sergeant Bleicher, the captive chief of Inter-Allied, said, "My name is Roman Czerniawski. I have done my duty".

Armand and Renée were taken into custody. So was the aged Madame Blavette, shrilly protesting that she had no knowledge of what had been taking place upstairs. She spent several months in jail, then was released when no connection could be found between Inter-Allied and Inter-Allied's landlady. Had she known there was a *Résistance* organization in her building? Of course.

Armand was handcuffed and taken immediately to the *Abwehr's* Paris headquarters at the Hotel Edouard VII, Avenue l'Opéra. Renée Borni, remaining at the apartment to dress, under Hugo Bleicher's interested and approving gaze, was devastated at the sudden disaster. She babbled like a terrified child, and under Hugo Bleicher's immensely solicitous and sympathetic questioning, Renée said this whole terrible affair was undoubtedly the work of her despised and vengeful rival, Mathilde Carré, who was due to arrive at the apartment about nine or ten o'clock, somewhat later, but regardless of that, "Everything has been her fault," exclaimed the distraught widow from Lunéville, "everything."

Renée finally finished dressing. Sergeant Bleicher scattered plainclothes *Abwehr* agent throughout the area, including the area of Avenue Cortot, then, with Renée at his side, went downstairs to wait.

Mathilde, who had spent the night at the Lejeune apartment, came forth in the morning to go to her own flat, despite a warning from Mirielle Lejeune that there had been German police sighted on the Avenue Junot, and that it would certainly be dangerous to be seen anywhere near 8 Villa Léandre.

Mathilde had gone anyway, her only comment on the possibility of danger being that if trouble was really imminent, she had at all risks to reach her room on the Avenue Cortot, because she had incriminating files, maps, and letters there, which had to be destroyed. She told Mirielle Lejeune that in the event she did not return, Mirielle was also to burn the papers Mathilde had left upstairs in the room where she had spent the night. Then she departed.

At the corner of her street, the Rue Cortot, Mathilde saw a number of men standing idly in the chill of this unpleasant damp, November morning. She walked right on past her residence, but, because she was the only pedestrian who had ever approached the building of her flat, the idling men, all *Abwehr* officers, followed her. One particular German pressed the pursuit. When Mathilde stopped to utilize a print shop window as a rear-view mirror, and saw the German approaching, she turned at once to resume walking. The German intercepted her and enquired what she was doing abroad so early in the morning. According to her own testimony later, in a French war-crimes court, Mathilde told the German she was looking for a gift among the local shops, for a friend she was to have luncheon with. The German then said, "Why don't you have lunch with me instead?" and Mathilde, who had encouraged propositions of this nature from Germans very often, by her own admission, and knew exactly how to counteract them, now turned without a word and walked swiftly back in the direction of her room on the Avenue Cortot.

The German resumed his pursuit. When Mathilde passed a

high fence, two *Abwehr* officers stepped forth, seized her by both arms, and hustled her to a nearby police van.

Mathilde's captors took her to the house on the Avenue Junot where the patient Sergeant Bleicher was waiting, with Renée Borni at his side. When the van stopped, Bleicher wordlessly opened a door in order that Renée would see the prisoner, then waited. Renée nodded vehemently, saying, "Yes, that's the Cat. That's her."

Both women were taken to the Hotel Edouard VII where they were briefly questioned about their personal background by an *Abwehr* clerk, this questioning presaging incarceration at the women's prison of La Santé. Renée whimpered in abject terror. Mathilde, who had sat stonily silent throughout the ride to *Abwehr* headquarters, did not show emotion as she was registered as a German prisoner. Later, both women, and Armand, were taken away, he, to Fresnes Prison, the two women to La Santé.

Sergeant Bleicher had assessed his captives. He was a very good judge of men; that had been demonstrated. Now, Bleicher was to demonstrate how qualified he was at judging the character of women.

Renée Borni, of course, was no challenge. And equally obvious, she was too patently simple for the people of Inter-Allied ever to have trusted her with much in the way of critical information. But the rounded, and voluptuous, sturdy woman in the red hat and black coat, was different. She was a challenge to Hugo Bleicher.

As before, he was in no great hurry. The nightmare experience of a sojourn in La Santé could do two-thirds of his work for him.

Armand, or as he was to be known again Captain Roman Czerniawski, was clearly not going to co-operate. Like Bernard Krutki, Bleicher's latest Polish captive was an unyielding man. But Sergeant Bleicher did not have to agonize over Czerniawski. He had Czerniawski's women.

It was a bitter November, the early winter of 1941. La Santé was not without heat, except in the cells of recalcitrant prisoners. Mathilde's recollection of her first unforgettable night at La Santé was stark. "I lay down on my bed fully dressed even in my . . . coat. I was so cold. I began to realize my situation; everything was finished, everything was destroyed. . . . So this was how my life was finishing – and I wanted to die . . . but not . . . [to] stay in prison . . . it was an impossibility that I should have to stay here . . . it was out of the question for me to stay in a place like that. Why, the water-closet smelled quite abominably."

8
Volte Face

Prison fare was commensurate with prison housing. Also, along with the bitter cold of very early morning, after Mathilde's sleepless terrible night, there was the nauseating stench.

She was ordered to clean her cell, she was fed a meagre breakfast of bad black coffee in a dented, unclean tin canister, and by sunrise her revulsion had reached its peak.

The Germans sent a car for her. From La Santé she was taken again to the Hotel Edouard VII, but this time Sergeant Bleicher had gone to considerable pains to create an atmosphere as different from that of La Santé as night was from day.

Mathilde was taken to an upstairs room, which was blessedly heated. She was permitted to wash, to become comfortable and at ease. Then breakfast arrived. There was sugar, and even butter. Cream for her coffee, linen, and immaculate utensils.

There was also Sergeant Bleicher, with a cigarette when she had finished eating, and a light. He was also an excellent conversationalist, never loud, profane, or abusive. This morning Bleicher was no different. He chatted a while, then mentioned that the *Abwehr* had all the papers from Mathilde's apartment, including her little appointment book, which also served as a diary. Also, he told Mathilde, the *Abwehr* not only had Armand, his entire map, file, and roster list, it also knew from Mathilde's little book, that she was familiar with every Inter-Allied agent who visited Armand's headquarters.

Bleicher had names, code-names and genuine names, but what he needed was someone who knew these spies and saboteurs by sight. For example, he said, the Germans had noted in Mathilde's little book that on this very day, 19th

November, she had an appointment to meet a certain man at a certain café at eleven o'clock in the morning. Bleicher had only a code-name. He laughed. Even an *Abwehr* official could not arbitrarily go about asking everyone he saw in or near a particular café if his name was such-and-such. Obviously then, since Inter-Allied had been thoroughly penetrated and would never function again, and Mathilde's former lover, Czerniawski, who had treated her so badly after all she had done to help him create his espionage organization, and who was not only an *Abwehr* captive, but would certainly implicate Mathilde, now that he would need a scapegoat ... now that he held her in contempt, in comparison with his latest lover, Renée Borni, she owed him nothing.

It was all there, everything Hugo Bleicher knew about 'the Cat' from files, correspondence, even her own journal, and Bleicher knew exactly how to use every bit of it. According to Mathilde's published memoirs – *J'ai este La Chatte*, Editions Morgan, Paris, 1959, Sergeant Bleicher said: "... we will work together ... and if you make no trouble for me, be assured that you will be free this evening. But if you deceive me, you will be executed at once, without a trial. ... Understand that England has lost. What is it they have been paying you? Six thousand francs a month? Of course; the English always make other people do their work for them. Nor do they even pay them properly. ... Believe me, Germany has won this war. Germany cannot lose. Those who oppose us will lose not just the war but their lives."

Concerning the café appointment, which was due to take place very shortly after their talk this morning of 19th November, 1941, Bleicher said: "I will accompany you as a member of your organization; you will introduce me as such, and when this spy has talked enough, I will arrest him. We will work together you and I. ..."

For Mathilde Carré the choices were exactly as they had been in Cherbourg for Raoul Kiffer. Collaboration or death, the latter to conceivably be imposed, after torture.

"... If you deceive me, you will be executed at once, without a trial. .." Those were the key words for Mathilde Carré. ... "England has lost." But there were also Bleicher's other remarks, made after his very careful study of Mathilde's notes: Armand had used her, had taken all she had given, and had obviously all the while been dreaming of the other woman, Renée, the widow of Lunéville. In the end, when he no longer needed Lily Carré, he had sent for the woman he had all the while really cared for. Not only Armand, but all the others who knew of this affair, privately laughed; Mathilde had been a dupe, a fool.

"Work loyally with me," he told her, "and you shall be free." The clear implication was that those others, faithless Armand, contemptible Renée, all the ones who had secretly smiled their contempt, would now pay dearly.

Finally, Bleicher said, "Do we understand each other?"

Mathilde's reply was, "I understand perfectly . . .".

Bleicher then took Mathilde to her rendezvous with the presumed secret agent. Bleicher, in civilian clothing, rode in the rear seat of an unmarked *Abwehr* car, complete with French licence plates, driven by another *Abwehr* man, in plain clothes.

At the café, the man who eventually approached Mathilde, and to whom Sergeant Bleicher was introduced as a fellow conspirator, "a trusted friend", was in fact not a member of Inter-Allied at all. He was instead a member of Vichy's *Deuxième Bureaux*. His name was Duverney, and what he wanted from Mathilde was information concerning German installations which could be passed along to the *Maquis*, the *Résistance*.

Sergeant Bleicher listened, and when he had heard enough, he invited Mathilde and her friend outside to his car. When all three were comfortable in the rear seat, Bleicher addressed Duverney quietly: "Monsieur, you are in the car of the German police, and you are under arrest." The ashen Frenchman was taken to the Hotel Edouard VII and delivered to the *Abwehr's* interrogators.

It was still early in the day, and Hugo Bleicher had only just begun. He knew that Mathilde was in the habit of telephoning her mother quite often, and in the off-chance that Madame Belard might be involved with Inter-Allied, Bleicher, who wanted everything to appear absolutely normal, took Mathilde to a public telephone at the Hotel Edouard VII, and, listening to every word the two women said, allowed Mathilde to contact the residence on Rue des Gobelins.

Madame Belard was tearfully relieved; she had heard through Mirielle Lejeune that the Germans had taken Mathilde into custody. Everyone, exclaimed Madame Belard, had been terribly upset. And Uncle Marco was especially anxious, because Mathilde had not kept her luncheon engagement with him.

Mathilde reassured her mother, and put down the telephone. Sergeant Bleicher pointed. She must now telephone Uncle Marco and explain that she had been unable to keep their appointment the previous day, but would be able to do so today.

Bleicher's insistence that everything must appear absolutely normal was about to pay an extra dividend, for with Bleicher listening, Uncle Marco, after expressing delight at hearing Mathilde's voice said he was to meet René Aubertin at the Café Graff at six o'clock that evening. "You must join us," he said to Mathilde, "and tell us what happened to you."

Mathilde promised to be there, rang off, and Bleicher, who already knew who René Aubertin was, from Armand's handwritten manuscript entitled *One Year Of Inter-Allied*, was delighted. But this rendezvous was not to take place until evening, and it was still only about mid-day.

True to the axiom that one should strike while the iron is hot, Bleicher loaded Mathilde into the unmarked car, once more, and took her for lunch to the Café La Palette, where Bernard Krutki had been apprehended. Subsequent to the arrest of Krutki, Bleicher had also taken the cloak-room crone, Madame Gaby, into custody. Then he had released her with a promise of immediate execution if she did not co-operate by acting in her regular capacity as the recipient of 'drops' by Inter-Allied agents. Madame Gaby, seeing Mathilde, whom she knew well, in the company of Hugo Bleicher, whom she also knew very well, was at a loss. In any event, when Bleicher asked what had arrived at the 'drop', Madame Gaby told him that nothing had arrived since the day before yesterday, so Bleicher and Mathilde proceeded to a table for lunch.

This was the first Mathilde knew of Bleicher's successful penetration of the Café La Palette drop. Everything that henceforth arrived for Madame Gaby's safe-keeping, would be promptly delivered to Hugo Bleicher, which meant, of course, that all Inter-Allied couriers not presently known to the *Abwehr*, and who had a Paris connection with the organization, would shortly be trapped.

Hugo Bleicher's bland explanation of the *Abwehr's* thoroughness impressed Mathilde, whose only experience with a clandestine organization had been with Inter-Allied. There was not really much of a comparison. The Germans were systematic, thorough, entirely professional. They had to be those things to succeed in an occupied country where not even their V-men really liked them. Inter-Allied, on the other hand, had, from start to finish, been operated as though espionage were a game, and except for the nationwide French antipathy, Inter-Allied would most probably never have lasted a year. There was also another comparison to be made. The comparison between Armand and Hugo Bleicher was to compare Cardinal Wolsey to one of his contemporary poets, or to compare "the Moor" Walsingham, with the seasick, but quite likeable, Spanish admiral of the Armada, Medina Sidonia. It was the difference, not only of temperament and character, but of experience and inherent capability. Armand was the romantic, the idealist, as opposed to Bleicher the pragmatist, the man of practical application, of cold reason. Armand, the man of vanity, opposed to Bleicher the realist. Bleicher was never as much a Nazi as he was an energetic competitor. It really only mattered very little to Hugo Bleicher whether he competed with Armand, or Erich Borchers, it only mattered that he competed, and that he triumphed.

For Mathilde the distinction was probably not that abstruse; Armand had been romantic, dashing, heroic, and masculinely attractive to her. Bleicher represented a great and seemingly triumphant, and irresistable, evil. Once, she had said, "What must be done; survive of course", and that was, again, the crux of it – survive.

At lunch with Bleicher that day Mathilde had already betrayed one Frenchman when the German finally paid their bill and led Mathilde out to the unmarked car, and said they would now proceed to apprehend 'Boby Roland' of the Paris police, and his wife Mirielle, Mathilde's close friend for almost a year, she did not offer one syllable of dissent.

They arrived outside the Lejeune residence on the Avenue Lamarck, and Mathilde, affectionately called 'Micheline' by Mirielle Leujeune, went to the door and knocked. Mirielle, with no idea the rather plain, unprepossessing-looking man with the thick-lensed glasses, was a German of the *Abwehr*, opened the door, and warmly welcomed Mathilde into her parlour. The man, Mathilde introduced as she had done to the Vichy-Frenchman; an acquaintance who could be trusted.

Mathilde asked what Mirielle had done with the papers she had left upstairs. Mirielle replied that she had burned them. Mathilde then somewhat erratically pointed to a vase of flowers which had also been upstairs, and demanded to know why Mirielle had taken them from Mathilde's upstairs room. Mirielle was nonplussed. Of what possible importance were the flowers? Then Mathilde asked to be given the Inter-Allied funds in Mirielle' possession, and the moment Mirielle got the money and handed it to Mathilde, Bleicher arrested her. Mirielle was stunned. It had never entered her mind that Mathilde's companion could be a German. While she stood speechless, Sergeant Bleicher asked Mirielle where her husband was.

Mirielle said, finally, that she did not know where her husband might be working this particular day, which was partly true; he was very often assigned to different areas of the city. Bleicher accepted this statement as calmly as he accepted most things, and also as he customarily did, he knew the solution.

He took Mirielle and Mathilde back to the car. They drove away to begin a round of visits of police installations. Bleicher sat in the rear with a woman on each side of him. Mathilde did not look at Mirielle, and did not speak to her.

They did not locate Mirielle's husband at the first police office, nor the second or third one, but finally 'Boby Roland' was found to be at the administrative Police establishment on the Champs Elysees. He was taken into custody, and together

with his wife, was also delivered, as the Vichy-Frenchman
Duverney had been, to the *Abwehr's* interrogaters at the Hotel
Edouard VII.

(Subsequently, Mirielle survived the war. She was freed
after less than a year of internment at La Santé. Her husband
did not survive, although he managed to live right up until
Germany collapsed – then died of malnutrition and excessive
abuse at Mathausen, one of the Third Reich's notorious
prisoner-of-war camps.)

Sergeant Bleicher's successes for this one day were
impressive, and he was not yet finished. By the time the search
for Inspector Lejeune had been satisfactorily concluded and he
and his wife had been delivered to the Paris headquarters of the
Abwehr, it was getting along towards early evening. The
rendezvous at the Café Graff was due to occur at six o'clock.

This time, however, Sergeant Bleicher had no illusions
about his adversaries being too stunned to react. He had two
carloads of military policemen come along. They, and
Bleicher, parked a discreet distance away. Bleicher told
Mathilde to go ahead, that he would follow after shortly.
Then he positioned his plain-clothes men so that anyone
entering the café, could do so quite unimpeded, but no one
could leave. Then, finally, Sergeant Bleicher, accompanied by
several plain-clothes men, went along to the café. The bar,
where Mathilde was to meet René and Uncle Marco, was on
the second floor. Uncle Marco was there exactly at six o'clock,
the first to arrive, excluding Mathilde. He greeted her with a
delighted hug. He, too, had heard she had been taken into
custody by the Germans.

Sergeant Bleicher had several of his plain-clothes
policemen take seats at the bar and order drinks, while
Bleicher took his position at a small table nearer the door.

Finally, René arrived, and because he had heard that
Mathilde was in German custody, and had not been informed
otherwise this afternoon, he was flabbergasted to see her
sitting at a little table in lively conversation with Marc
Marchal. Charles Lejeune himself had warned René Aubertin
that Mathilde had been apprehended. He recovered from the
surprise as he approached the table. When Uncle Marco
beamed a smile, and Mathilde raised her eyes, also smiling,

René said, "But how can you be here? I was told you were in the hospital."

Mathilde's reply was calm and pleasant. "Sit down, and I will explain."

René ordered three aperitifs, sat down, and when Mathilde said, "Why are you so upset?" René explained about Charles Lejeune's statement concerning her arrest, and he also said that Charles Lejeune had warned René that something very bad appeared to be occurring. Mathilde passed this off with a light comment. "Boby Roland did not really understand what was happening. Later, I will explain it all to you. Enjoy your drink."

Aubertin could not rid himself of a bad feeling, a premonition. He did not touch the highball glass – not then, but a few moments later he did.

Bleicher signalled the plain-clothes men at the bar. They turned at once and approached the table where Mathilde and her friends sat. René Aubertin and Uncle Marco had their first inkling of trouble when two of the Germans pressed pistols into their backs, while another plain-clothes man announced that he and his companions were members of the German police, and that the two Frenchmen were under arrest.

"If you move," one of the Germans said, "we will shoot you."

Bleicher watched all this from his table near the door. Very few of the bar's other patrons had any idea what had happened. Mathilde looked as though she would faint, and both her companions thought this was her reaction to being arrested. They had no idea that it was she who had helped organize their capture. That realization would come soon enough.

When the shock had passed, and the prisoners were ordered to arise and quietly depart with their captors, René Aubertin reached in a pocket for money to pay for the drinks, then solemnly raised all three glasses, one at a time, and downed their contents under the impassive eyes of the Germans.

It was just as well. He would not have another highball for almost four years.

The two Frenchmen were taken by *Abwehr* car to the same

chamber of interrogation at the Hotel Edouard VII which had
also accommodated Mirielle and Charles Lejeune and the
Vichy-Frenchman, Duverney. Hugo Bleicher had managed to
conclude a very successful day. But it was not quite complete,
just yet. There remained another residence on the Avenue
Lamarck to be visited. Mathilde directed the *Abwehr* chauffeur
back to Montmartre once again, to the residence of that
couple from Alsace, the Hugentoblers, whose residence had
served Inter-Allied from time to time as a 'drop', where
informers left information to be picked up by couriers.
Mathilde had very often been the courier. When she arrived at
the Hugentoblers' flat, Madame was preparing dinner. She
was a large, emotional, very strong family person, happiest at
this moment of the day surrounded by her family. Besides
Monsieur Hugentobler, there was a daughter of fourteen, and
a baby of less than a year. Madame was happy that evening. It
was an impossibility that by morning she would be dead.

Sergeant Bleicher entered the apartment one step behind
Mathilde. To the astonished Hugentoblers, who of course
recognised Mathilde, the shock was as great as it had been at
the Café Graff for Uncle Marco and René Aubertin when
Bleicher said, "You are under arrest – *Police Allemande!*"

The man stood transfixed with astonishment. His wife, a
good soul, a domestic woman without guile, reacted with an
outcry. She could not go! She had her baby, and her other
daughter. Bleicher was adamant. Madame turned in tears to
Mathilde, crying for 'Micheline' to explain, to intercede.

Mathilde stood against a wall watching and saying nothing.
The Hugentoblers were taken away. A German stood between
the hysterical older daughter and the mother. To every
importunity directed to Hugo Bleicher, he said, "France will
look after your children".

The Hugentoblers were also taken to the *Abwehr's* Paris
headquarters, the Hotel Edouard VII. Bleicher's first day in
consort with Mathilde Carré was now finished. For Sergeant
Bleicher it had been a day to remember in triumph. He had
brought to heel a French Brigadier of police, the Brigadier's
wife, a former French tank officer, Aubertin – in fact two
former French tank officers, Marc Marchal had been a tanker

in the first German war – a commercial chemist, the same Marc Marchal, a Vichy Frenchman, a traitor to Petain and the Germans, and two Alsations, the Hugentoblers, the woman who had become increasingly bereft and irresponsible, until, shortly after being thrown in a cell at La Santé, she put everyone's nerves on edge with her shrill outcries for her baby.

Best of all, Bleicher still had Mathilde, the source of all his good fortune. She knew many more of the French who had collaborated with the British. She had volunteered to betray most of the people Bleicher now had in custody and would continue to volunteer.

One would escape, but it was a bitter escape. At La Santé, Madame Hugentobler, driven out of her mind with worry for her two parentless daughters, especially the youngest one, convinced she would never be reunited with her family again, hanged herself, and was discovered in the morning, dead.

She was the first to pay with her life for Mathilde's perfidy, but by no means was she to be the last.

9
Kleines Kätzchen

The capture of René Aubertin and Marc Marchal resulted for
both men in an odyssey of travail which was not novel among
the people Mathilde betrayed. Armand – Roman Czerniawski
– underwent a similar tribulation. After brutal interrogations
he was eventually sent to Mathausen, where he witnessed the
deaths of former friends and acquaintances, including the
slight and sensitive Polish aristocrat, Lucien de Roquigny,
who had been in love with Mathilde Carré. De Roquigny
collapsed as a result of being beaten, then was literally kicked
to death.

René Aubertin was initially taken to the Hotel Edouard
VII, as was Marc Marchal. After being questioned there, both
men were sent to Fresnes Prison. Again they were grilled,
more intensely this time.

Aubertin, Mathilde's childhood playmate, her supporter
during the difficult days after Armand had replaced her with
Renée Borni, existed at Fresnes Prison under conditions of
incredible hardship, then was transferred to Romainville to
become one of those hostages the Germans kept, like cattle, to
be used as examples, if sacrificial victims were required in
retaliation for underground attacks upon the conquerors. For
thirty days Aubertin waited hourly for the command to march
out to the execution area.

Finally, having survived Fresnes and Romainville, he was
transferred again, this time to the death camp at Mathausen.
Here, he was kept for over two years, his physical condition
steadily worsening until, with a lung infection which kept him
ill most of the time, Aubertin had to pretend he was in good
health in order to avoid being gassed and cremated as an
invalid unable to work.

A fellow prisoner, using a stolen syringe, daily drained fluid from the infected lung. In this way René Aubertin was able to survive. At the end of the war he was able to return to France, his health permanently impaired.

Marc Marchal – Uncle Marco – had a unique experience; he was saved from death by a German soldier. But before that occurred, he was held at Fresnes for half a year, treated harshly because he would not respond favourably to interrogations, then sent to Treves for torture. Here, along with the torture, Marchal was kept chained in a bitterly cold cell, without any light, for six months. He was then sent as an incorrigible recalcitrant to the notorious Buchenwald extermination facility, six miles from Weimar, a town noted as a shrine of German culture. Here, where for almost eight years prisoners were experimented on like guinea pigs by German surgeons, where people were literally drowned in manure, crushed to death under great stones, beaten to death, and shot to death by the thousand, Marchal, under setence of death, was allowed a respite because he was an accomplished chemist.

Instead of being killed, he was transferred to the great Neuengamme complex, a prison facility with no less than fifty-five satellite extermination facilities. At Neuengamme, almost a hundred thousand human beings passed through the camp between 1938, when Neuengamme was founded, and 1945 when it was closed down, and of that 100,000 prisoners, one-half, or very close to 50,000, died of beatings, starvation, exposure, or from medical experimentation.

It was here that Marc Marchal, the chemist, was offered his life in exchange for co-operating with German doctors who were conducting brutal surgical experiments oh prisoners. Marchal refused. He was then sent to Mathausen as a 'nacht und nebel' prisoner; someone to be put to death quickly and discreetly. There was no reprieve for this kind of prisoner.

Marchal arrived at Mathausen in the early hours of a very dark night. The SS officers had retired hours earlier. There was a grizzled *Wehrmacht* non-commissioned officer on duty. He was a former member of a tank regiment, as was Marchal. This information was in the dossier handed to the non-commissioned officer when Marchal was delivered to his office. The German read Marchal's record, removed the immediate execution order, then sent Marchal to a prisoner barracks. One former tanker had acknowledged the contributions of, and had saved the life of, another former tanker.

Marchal was subsequently assigned to the prison hospital at Mathausen, and although his own health steadily deteriorated, he was still struggling to save lives when the war ended.

He lived another five years, then died, completely worn out, and suffering the lingering effects of his prison-contracted, terminal maladies.

Those were only a few examples of what happened to the people Mathilde Carré betrayed to the Germans, through Hugo Bleicher, on her first day as a double agent, and when the final drama of that day occurred, Madame Hugentobler was still alive, while Armand, 'Uncle Marco', René Aubertin, Lucien de Roquigny, and the Vichy-Frenchman, Duverney, among others, were only just beginning to face what was, for each of them, an incredible revelation: the woman who had persuaded most of them to serve Inter-Allied, and the Allies, had deliberately betrayed them all.

The final episode of the day occurred shortly after Aubertin and Marchal were delivered to the Hotel Edouard VII. Hugo Bleicher drove Mathilde to a good restaurant for dinner. He was in excellent spirits, and in no hurry. After they had dined, Bleicher took Mathilde back to his car. She expected him to drive her to the room on the Avenue Cortot. Instead he drove in the direction of the *Abwehr* headquarters at Mason Lafitte. When she asked if Bleicher did not mean to keep his word, and set her free, he replied that, in fact, she was free. She was certainly not back at La Santé, where she had spent the previous night. Bleicher intended to take her to *Abwehr* St Germain, where she would be free, subject to a little German supervision, that was all. After all, Mathilde would very shortly be known as an ally of the Germans; she would need protection.

When she protested, Bleicher insisted that for her own sake, she must henceforth reside among her German friends. At *Abwehr* St Germain, he showed her to her room. Then, according to Mathilde's account, she "found herself in the presence of the most disgusting, sentimental beast". Perhaps, but Mathilde offered no recriminations, and no struggle. Later, at her trial, when asked by the French judge if it were necessary to go to bed that night with Sergeant Bleicher, Mathilde replied: "Well, what else could I have done?" When asked by the judge about the men she betrayed that day, Mathilde said: "There was nothing I could do about it . . . our agents made a great mistake in keeping their appointments with me."

The following morning Mathilde appeared downstairs at *Abwehr* St Germain, the only woman among German officers, jaunty, flirtatious, teasingly triumphant. They called her *Kleines Kätzchen*. Over the ensuing days she turned *Abwehr* St Germain into Madame Carré's *chambre d'amour*. The Germans were excellent hosts. She had as much adulation as she craved, and for the first time since diving into a ditch to avoid the *Stukas*, she was quite secure. The meals were good, the wine ample, and although she did not speak German, many of the Germans of *Abwehr* St Germain spoke French.

The German commander at St Germain, far from objecting to having a woman in his headquarters, kissed Mathilde's hand, joked and sang with her. The other men were equally as gallant. Sergeant Bleicher would play the piano. Mathilde said later that he "played remarkably well and could even improvise most tastefully". They would all gather round and sing.

Fresnes Prison, dead Madame Hugentobler, Mathausen and Neuengamme were not in the same world. For the Germans, the raging inferno of Russia was completely closed out. *Abwehr* St Germain was more than Mathilde had thought it could be. Its German staff, said Mathilde, "looked at me with a great deal of admiration".

Clearly, Mathilde had found a fresh source of the kind of inspiration, without which she could not be a complete person. Within a matter of a day or two, the same plan which had enabled her to abandon her husband at Toulouse in the Haute Garonne, through a needless act of petty treachery, had surfaced anew in an appalling way, and her conscience, which had not troubled her then, did not trouble her now.

She would have been content to be the *Kleines Kätzchen* of *Abwehr* St Germain without additional treachery. People like Mathilde, without conscience, do not appear as a rule to be highly motivated. Mathilde was no exception. She was entirely comfortable at Maison Lafitte. She was a prima donna of the *Abwehr*. She was also the quite willing bedfellow of Hugo Bleicher. But because she was content did not imply that Bleicher was.

Mathilde was still a valuable acquisition. It was true that after her betrayal of Inter-Allied's leadership, the organization was a headless dragon to the Germans, but smashing Inter-Allied simply meant that one espionage network had been crushed. It did *not* mean that the hundreds of French members of the satellite cells could not promptly find other networks to serve, and *this* was Bleicher's motivation – catch spies.

Mathilde knew dozens of underground *résistants*. Hugo Bleicher's creditable successes so far, for ambition's sake alone, could not be allowed to languish. It may have been, as has been said, that Sergeant Bleicher aspired to commissioned-officer status. Possibly – but basically Bleicher was a manhunter, and a very good one. Ambition would have been a corollary adjunct to his inherent manhunting instincts.

He enjoyed his mistress, naturally, Frau Bleicher being many miles distant, in a totally foreign atmosphere, but enjoying Mathilde's sensuality, exclusive of her other, less passionate, attributes, was never for a moment what Hugo Bleicher had in mind.

He ordered Mathilde's life pattern. They made ardent love at night, they went manhunting by day, and during the evenings they relaxed at the Villa Harry Bauer, playing the piano, singing, enjoying excellent wine and food, and Mathilde flirted, as she always had, with her entourage of admiring Germans. But Bleicher's zealous manhunting never for a moment allowed the interludes of pleasure to interfere with work.

She even took Bleicher to meet her parents at the Avenue des Gobelins. He was in civilian attire, as he commonly was when the two of them stalked *résistants*. They enjoyed lunch with the Belards, and despite a subsequent illusion to the

possibility that Madame and Monsieur did not realize that
their daughter's new companion was a German, later, at
Mathilde's trial in France, it was revealed that they had
known, that in fact neither Mathilde nor Bleicher made any
secret of it.

How did Monsieur Belard react? He held the Legion of
Honour decoration, and had survived a wound from the other
German war. He sat and related adventures from that other
war, then listened as Hugo Bleicher did the same, as a soldier
from the other side.

Bleicher said he had no use for the British, whose prisoner
he had been for a while during the First World War, but he
admired the French, respected their culture, and was in
sympathy with their current plight. He finally assured the
Belards that he would make certain that their daughter would
be safe and protected. The only contingency revolved around
the co-operation of Monsieur and Madame. They must help
protect Mathilde by being co-operative with Bleicher. But the
Belards actually knew very little – a little gossip, some dark
hints, but Mathilde had not confided in them in years, not
since marrying her schoolmaster and going out to North
Africa, and as for themselves, they did not go out much, did
very little entertaining or visiting. With conditions as they
were, it was not possible to entertain, food being as dear as it
was, moreover, they were not young people; much that was
now happening baffled them. They lived a quiet and orderly
life, and prayed often for their son, who was, God knew where,
perhaps in Africa, soldiering under De Gaulle.

Fatalism had always been endemic in the Gallic patrimony.
Madame did not like her daughter's present affiliation at all.
Monsieur, too, was saddened by it. They were not fools; the
French who collaborated with the conquerors of France,
regardless of how the cursed war ended, and regardless of
whether they actually aided the Germans or not, could not be
said to have been true to the ideals of France. On the other
hand, the Germans were there; they had won their war
against France. Those were the clear and unalterable facts of
life. In any direction they looked, there were Germans, and as
the daughter of Madame and Monsieur Belard had often said:

What was to be done? Well, obviously, survive.

It was more difficult for Madame, whose strong emotions, and female intuition encouraged a quick perception of Mathilde's relationship with Bleicher. For Monsieur the difficulty was less emotional but not less painful. He was a hero of France, with a son to be proud of and a daughter who had achieved an accommodation with the enemies of France.

The sum of thought and conjecture was survival. Disasteful though it was for the Belards and others like them by the hundreds of thousands, unable to serve actively with honour and too old to spend bitterly cold nights lying in ambushes, there was left simply an acceptance – a bitter but practical recognition, a genuine and passive fatalism.

This was the Belards' ultimate reaction, because there was no other. Mathilde could have interpreted it as passive acceptance by people she felt to be far beyond understanding – old people. Bleicher, lacking an emotional involvement, only viewed the elderly parents of his mistress as additional French people from which he might elicit either information or co-operation.

In any event the Belards did not share their daughter's life, which was fortunate, because it was then possible, without proof to the contrary, to believe what they chose to believe. Otherwise, there were all the 'conditions'. For sixteen months after Nazi Germany attacked through Poland, German arms achieved an unqualified success. Excluding the Battle of Britain, in which land armies had played no part, not one genuine reverse had impeded the Nazi juggernaut. The condition of France was undeniable; she had been beaten to her knees, and was now a captive. The condition of Germany was a study in triumph – and barbarity. The condition of the other occupied lands was, in many instances, worse even than the condition of France.

Britain had been mortally wounded, but refused to die. The United States worked day and night, creating an 'arsenal for democracy', but procrastinated otherwise. And now, for people of the Belard's generation, there was still another 'condition' to fumble with.

Germany's attack upon Soviet Russia in mid 1941,

spearheaded by 6000 guns and 2700 tanks, stunned the world.
Within forty-eight hours the Russians lost two thousand
aircraft. Within eighteen days German troops penetrated to
the Leningrad province. They had advanced at the rate of
fifty miles a day. Within three weeks they were half a
thousand miles into the Soviet Union, and had 300,000 Soviet
prisoners. Ten days later they had 100,000 more captives.
They were by then only two hundred miles from Moscow.

The condition of Russia was obviously moribund. In
September, two German commands, those of Guderian and
von Runstedt, in one operation, destroyed and captured a
Russian force of 600,000 men, and in the first week of October
Reichsführer Hitler announced to the world "without any
reservation", that the Soviet Union had been "struck down
and will never rise again".

What, then, were people like the Belards to believe?
Lacking the indomitable will of the young, completely
overwhelmed by conditions which clearly indicated that, this
time, the Germans could not be beaten, saddened, of course,
and living between two worlds, their own senescent era of a
much earlier, more leisurely time, and this terribly
bewildering world of Mathilde, in which catastrophes
occurred between luncheon and dinner, between bedtime and
awakening, perhaps Mathilde was right and they were wrong.
Perhaps Mathilde's Germans would triumph utterly.

If this were to happen, then Mathilde would not be seen as
a traitor, but as a clever woman of uncommon prescience. In
mid and late 1941, not only the Belards had this optional view
available to them, but it was for the grey and worried parents
of Mathilde, a very strong possibility, and they chose to abide
by it. They had every reason but one, to want to abide by it,
their son, a French officer of the fighting French forces.

10
La Chatterie

Hugo Bleicher's itinerary during those first days of Mathilde's betrayals did not vary. He would get the name, status, address, and as much of the background of each Inter-Allied agent as Mathilde knew, from her, then he would take her in his car and set out, usually with a carload of *Abwehr* men following along, to make the arrest.

Bleicher moved discreetly as well as swiftly. He did not want London to realize that German penetration of one of SOE's best espionage networks had been achieved, and while it was not possible to prevent the knowledge from becoming extant that something most certainly had gone wrong, his discreet apprehensions were engineered so that the people he took into custody were quickly taken to prison, where they could not communicate with former friends and associates of the underground.

In those times of extravagant rumours, of every kind of covert duplicity, of great confusion and very little actual or factual knowledge, Bleicher's *modus operandi* was certain to be successful, and it was. But there was also danger. Men such as Aubertin and Marchal were not susceptible to German persuasion. They were always armed, and by 1941 when *Abwehr*, Gestapo and *Geheime Feldpolizei* activity had become quite proficient, Frenchmen of the underground, knowing their fate if captured, had begun to demonstrate a willingness to shoot it out with the Germans rather than to surrender peaceably.

Mathilde was able to brief Bleicher on the personality and character of the people she helped him apprehend. As an example, the tall, lean, dark Pole, 'Rapide', who had served Inter-Allied so well as a courier and infiltrator, was known to be a cool, courageous, and deadly man. His correct name was

Stanislas Lach. He was an excellent mechanic, among other things, and had at one time been employed at the Citroen works in Paris. He was married and lived in a small, third-floor apartment of the Ile St Louis area, on the rue des Deux Ponts, with a pleasant little courtyard fronting his flat, below.

Hugo Bleicher, who by now knew that Inter-Allied's Polish members were in touch with Colonel Vincent Zarembski's Tudor network at Toulouse and Marseilles, was eager to capture an Inter-Allied courier, such as 'Rapide', who could help him penetrate the other network. Inevitably, penetration of one network led to the uncovering of other *réseaux*, and their parent organization.

Mathilde had cautioned Bleicher about Lach: he was not a man German soldiers could walk up to and simply arrest, therefore, although Bleicher had along his carload of armed *Abwehr* men, he did not do as he had done elsewhere – go charging in, gun drawn – instead, he positioned his men discreetly out of sight, except for one soldier which he kept with him, then he sent Mathilde up the stairs first, while he, with a gun in each hand, and his companion, also armed and ready, remained behind, and below, as Mathilde went upstairs and knocked on the door.

Stanislas Lach and his wife were eating their noon meal. When he opened the door and recognized his caller, Lach and his wife invited her in to eat with them. They suspected nothing. They knew something had happened to Inter-Allied, but they had no idea Mathilde was responsible.

Mathilde stood in the open doorway. She declined the offer of lunch and told Lach that something had happened to Armand, and that she must at once alert both London and Marseilles, but she did not know how to reach Tudor in the French seaport city.

Lach stood gazing at her. If anyone should have known how to contact the Tudor network, it should have been Armand's confidant of almost a full year's duration.

Lach said, "I thought you had visited Tudor at Marseilles."

Mathilde replied that she had not, and that she must have the address immediately, as there was great danger.

Stanislas Lach was disturbed as much by Mathilde's

peculiar nervous attitude, as by her statement that she did not
know how to contact the Polish network, with which all of
Inter-Allied's leadership had been in touch, at one time or
another.

Gradually, as they stood facing one another at the open
doorway, Lach became suspicious. Mathilde made a few more
statements, her manner becoming increasingly agitated, then
she abruptly turned to descend the stairs.

Bleicher, with a weapon in each hand, in the best Wild
West tradition, rushed forward, pushed Mathilde back
through the doorway, and as the second German crowded
forward, also with a gun in his hand, Bleicher ordered all
three people, Lach, his wife, and Mathilde, to get against the
wall with their arms raised.

At the time, Stanislas Lach did not suspect Mathilde's part
in his capture. Bleicher's deliberate roughness with her was of
course convincing. He did not want anyone to know that she
was his double agent.

He succeeded, as usual. Lach and his terrified wife had to
stand by while more Germans appeared, and ransacked the
apartment. What they found, verified Mathilde's judgment of
the lanky Pole; two loaded pistols and a phial of strychnine.

Bleicher then took his captives, including Mathilde, playing
her part well, down to the *Abwehr* vehicles. As the prisoners
were put in the back, Bleicher and his *Abwehr* chauffeur up
front, Lach pieced things together, and said to Mathilde, "You
have done a fine job today". He got no response.

At the Hotel Edouard VII the prisoners, Lach and his wife,
were taken away to be interrogated. Mathilde saw them both
for the last time that afternoon, for although both Lach and his
wife survived the war – he spent years in prison, was tortured
repeatedly, and was half dead at Mathausen, when Allied
armies sweeping through Germany, released him – their paths
did not cross again.

The *Abwehr* took over Inter-Allied's Ville Léandre
command post, staffed it with knowledgeable counter-
intelligence men, who were both bilingual and briefed on all
that the Germans knew of the organization, and in this
manner trapped a number of quite unsuspecting agents,

including a number of couriers bringing information to headquarters from the outlying cells.

All this was done within a few days of Armand's capture, and of Mathilde's *volte face*, which was exactly as Hugo Bleicher had composed his capture-strategy. He also had something in mind which could conceivably devastate all espionage networks in Occupied France – penetration on a scale that could possibly reach all the way to London.

Lucien – 'Paul' – de Roquigny, who died at Mathausen under the savage circumstances previously related, was captured in the same manner that Bleicher apprehended Stanislas Lach. Mathilde went to de Roquigny's flat close by the Boulevard St Michel, and knocked on the door. When de Roquigny opened the door and recognized Mathilde, he invited her in. Bleicher rushed in, gun in hand.

Mathilde smoked a cigarette in the vestibule until the Germans completed their customary ransacking and came forth with their prisoner. De Roquigny paused, momentarily, to gaze at the woman he understood now had betrayed him, then smiled at her and was hustled out to an *Abwehr* car, destined never to return.

Hugo Bleicher had a stroke of good fortune at de Roquigny's quarters. He came upon the Paris address of Armand's former map and information co-ordinator, Wladimir Lipsky, whose residence on a hill in Montmartre was shared by Lipsky's teen-age daughter, Cipinka.

Lipsky would, in Bleicher's view, be another very worthwhile acquisition. There was enough known about him, by now, for the *Abwehr* to consider Lipsky a tough and resourceful enemy. For example, he had aided British Intelligence in the First World War, for another thing, Lipsky had made no secret of his fierce and enduring hatred of the Germans – after they had shot his wife to death during the invasion of Poland in 1939. Finally, the maps, files, and records, now in German hands, from Inter-Allied's headquarters, showed evidence of a very competent and masterful hand at work in their maintenance, not to mention their accuracy.

The routine still did not vary. Bleicher, Mathilde, and the

carload of *Abwehr* men appeared at Lipsky's flat. Mathilde
knocked, and when Wladimir Lipsky opened the door,
Bleicher was there too, gun in hand. During Lipsky's
subsequent grilling at Fresnes, the Germans repeatedly struck
him in the face. His nose was broken, his eyes were swollen
closed, and all his teeth were knocked out.

Subsequently, he too, along with his daughter, was sent to
Mathausen. They both were liberated by American troops in
1945, Lipsky an invalid for the rest of his life.

Bleicher did not rest, but from this point on, from the vast
amount of information gleaned from Inter-Allied's files, and
such other incriminating documents as Armand's journal,
Mathilde's diary, and carelessly kept scraps of paper with
names and addresses upon them, such as de Roquigny's
memo on Lipsky, Bleicher could round up spies, couriers,
informers, and saboteurs, without taking Mathilde along each
time. He could, in fact, send out details of men from *Abwehr* St
Germain to make some of the apprehensions, without his
having to accompany them.

While the Germans were quite satisfied that the Paris police
bureaux harboured a number of sympathisers with the
underground, and even a great many activists, these men were
by training and experience as thoroughly adept at subterfuge
as were the Germans, and in consequence, rooting out
particular anti-German policemen was difficult.

Bleicher's success in this area was accomplished largely
without any assistance from Mathilde, but he had learned a
few things subsequent to the arrest of Inspector Charles
Lejeune, which enabled him to go personally, and also to
dispatch other *Abwehr* elements, to make arrests.

Bleicher did not always succeed. As yet, the underground
did not know that Mathilde was a double agent, but it
required no vast degree of perspicacity to understand that
something was very wrong. Once, when Bleicher set up a
rendezvous, with Mathilde as co-conspirator, and bait, to
entice agents and couriers from other networks and outlying
cells, only one very minor courier walked into the trap. People
did not know that Mathilde was a double agent for the
Germans, but they did realize that the Germans were

becoming increasingly efficient, and avoided them at all costs.

Bleicher once failed to entrap a radio operator (called "musicians" among the networks). This happened when the operator became suspicious at the last moment and eluded capture by turning back, when the Germans had him in sight.

Still, Bleicher's confidence in the value of Mathilde remained strong. A few small failures, as well as the fact that the diminishing arrests of Inter-Allied's agents, the direct result of so many being captured with Mathilde's help, simply meant that Hugo Bleicher had fairly well dried up one source of fodder for the concentration camps, and must shortly now develop new sources, and that brought him face to face with the idea he had been considering for some time now. It was not an original thought in the field of counter-Intelligence, but at least among the Germans, it had never achieved very many notable successes. It would succeed for Bleicher, though, because he had the full support and cooperation of his knowledgeable 'paramour', to make it succeed.

Up until now, Bleicher, and the man who ranked him, but who otherwise was not his equal, Captain Erich Borchers, had done almost nothing about Inter-Allied's shortwave contact with London. Also, as long as they, and Mathilde, were residents of the *Abwehr* facility at Villa Bauer they were somewhat restricted by the work of other *Abwehr* agents, who shared those facilities. It was Bleicher's idea to obtain a separate facility which would be dedicated exclusively to developing a wider scope for Mathilde's talents, and for broadening their counter-Intelligence base to include an attempt at penetrating British Intelligence through radio contact with S.O.E., French Section, which was, by late 1941, a major source of support and supply of the French underground.

From this point forward, as a result of the acquisition of that mass of incriminating information acquired through the penetration and destruction of the Inter-Allied network, other *Abwehr* officers could glean what they needed to press the manhunt. (They did it so well, as 1941 neared its end, that the two prisons, La Santé for women, Fresnes for men, were soon full.) This freed Hugo Bleicher, Mathilde Carré, and Captain

Erich Borchers for the fresh strategy Bleicher had been considering for some time.

Bleicher secured an appointment with Colonel Oscar Reile, commandant of Bleicher's section of *Abwehr III*, in Paris, and made a proposal which, up to 1941, had not been tried by the Germans in the Second World War. He told Colonel Reile that he now had four Inter-Allied transmitters, all tuned to the London wavelengths. He was reasonably certain that, so far, S.O.E., F-Section, did not realize that Inter-Allied had been destroyed. "We can", he told Reile, "... make London believe that Inter-Allied functions as before. In this way we can get all the signals and instructions from British Intelligence, all news about the despatch of secret agents from London, and we can send them false information in return."

Colonel Reile was sceptical. Clandestine radio operators had elaborate and foolproof systems for thwarting compulsory transmissions. Bleicher had the remedy for that; he told the colonel that his double agent, Mathilde Carré, could persuade former Inter-Allied agents to transmit faithfully. Colonel Reile's doubts did not diminish, but he agreed to allow the effort to be made. His approval made it possible for the first 'turned-around' radio of the war to function, but, although Reile had faith in Sergeant Bleicher, he put others in command. Baron von Hoeffel was to be commandant. Major Eschig, commandant of *Abwehr* St Germain, was to exercise local supervision, while two non-commissioned officers Tritsch and Probst, the latter being an experienced telegrapher, along with a dark, Levantine-looking man, Dr Kaiser, completed the staff. There were to be others, but not just yet.

A separate facility was to be established, separate from, but in the same general locale as, *Abwehr* St Germain. Accordingly, the residence of a wealthy French businessman at St Germain-en-Laye, was commandeered. It was rather a handsome house, known as 'The Little Priory'. It had a ground floor, a second floor with three bedrooms and a bath, and on the third floor there was room for the establishment of the radio equipment.

The house had a timbered façade, resembling to some extent English Elizabethan architecture. There was a pleasant little balcony opening off the second floor, in front. Altogether, the house was quite pleasant. It had central heating, a bar in a corner of one of the downstairs rooms, its own private garden, and a degree of seclusion.

Here, Bleicher brought the captured transmitter from Villa Léandre. Here, too, he and Mathilde established themselves in one of the upstairs bedrooms, while the other Germans were compelled to either crowd into other rooms, or sleep elsewhere. Then Bleicher did as Armand had also done, but from entirely different motives; he had Renée Borni brought to the house. Renée had coded most of Inter-Allied's messages to London. Getting her to do the same for the *Abwehr* posed no problems. She agreed to work for the Germans in exchange for the basic comforts of everyday life, but she and Mathilde still detested each other, and while they usually refused to speak, or to even look at one another, there were occasional flare-ups, and when these occurred the Germans sent Renée out of the room.

Bleicher now had to resolve the critical matter of a trustworthy radio operator. There was a Frenchman, code-named 'Marcel', of the Inter-Allied organization, who had become disenchanted some months earlier, and had left. His real name, Mathilde remembered, had been Henri Tabet. A search was instituted for this man, and meanwhile Bleicher visited Inter-Allied's other former wireless operators. All the Poles refused flatly to cooperate.

Bleicher could have taken a chance, and employed a German operator. The reason this was only considered as a last resort, was related to the unique designation of "musician" for wireless operators. Each one had as distinctive a touch on the telegraph key as a musical virtuoso. London, after so many months of intimate contact with Inter-Allied's operators, would almost certainly have recognized a new hand and, would have also with almost equal certainty, become justifiably suspicious.

Despite Bleicher's lack of success with former Inter-Allied wireless operators, he was not required to resort to the last alternative, because 'Marcel' was eventually tracked down by *Abwehr* agents, and arrested. As with others, including Raoul Kiffer and Claude Jouffret, Henry Tabet, as 'Marcel' of Inter-Allied, had a simple choice to make; co-operate or be executed.

Tabet chose the less final solution; he agreed to transmit for the Germans exactly as he had for Inter-Allied.

Bleicher's *ménage* was now complete. It only lacked one thing; a name. At Bleicher's suggestion the house at St Germain-en-Laye, was called *La Chatterie*, the cattery. Mathilde was flattered. She was also vindictively delighted to have Renée Borni, the dense widow of Lunéville, told of this fresh honour.

Finally, with all in readiness, Bleicher, Borchers, and the German sergeants who would be directly supervising radio transmissions, had to devise safe-guards which would prevent their collaborators, including Mathilde, from somehow warning London that the resumed Inter-Allied transmissions were not genuine. A rather elaborate system of paper-shuffling was evolved. The Germans would write down what they wished to have transmitted. Mathilde would then rewrite the message in her distinctive variety of French. This message would then be given to Renée, who would make changes in the coding, after which it would be again re-arranged by the Germans, and handed to 'Marcel' for Transmission, under the close supervision of the German telegrapher, who sat with a jamming key in hand to interrupt the message at any point Marcel might attempt a change, or an addition.

It worked, but actually the British had already in use a very simple method of detecting compulsory or imitation messages by simply transposing a harmless word in a message, or by mis-spelling a pre-arranged word. The reason messages initiated at the Cattery did not contain any of the keys which would have warned London, was simply because Henri Tabet – 'Marcel' – did not employ them. He co-operated as satisfactorily as did Mathilde.

There was another detail requiring attention: Inter-Allied had not been in contact with London for some time, and there was an excellent possibility, too, that someone, perhaps the radio operator who had escaped over the roof-tops when Armand had been captured at the Ville Léandre, had sent a message to S.O.E. about the Germans raiding Inter-Allied's headquarters.

These two matters were jointly resolved. A plausible story

was concocted. Over the Cat's signature it was decided to tell London that, as a matter of fact, Armand and 'Violette', the code-clerk – Renée Borni – had been captured in the raid on Inter-Allied's headquarters, which very deftly took care of the possible warning sent London by the escaped telegrapher.

As for the delay in transmissions, the Cat would explain that, by saying the raid on the Ville Léandre had temporarily created a disruption, and up until now, the Cat had been unable to resume transmitting, had been compelled to go into hiding, temporarily, but was now prepared to resume the work of the organization.

It was all quite plausible, but of course until London called back, with some kind of tangible guarantee, such as the promise of an air-drop of funds, arms, or, best of all, secret agents and more radio equipment, no one at either the Cattery or *Abwehr* St Germain would be able to say that Hugo Bleicher's scheme was a success.

These plans were not entirely Bleicher's. Mathilde refined them for him on the basis of what she alone already knew of Inter-Allied's contacts with London. Bleicher, even with all Inter-Allied's records of previous messages available to him, could not have known the nuances. Mathilde alone knew these.

11

'Victoire'

When the scheme to dupe British Intelligence was perfected, Mathilde Carré, whose code-name 'the Cat' had appeared on so many messages, was of the opinion that it would look more plausible if she did not use that code-name now. Her reasoning was that if she were really in hiding, with the Germans monitoring their air waves looking for her, she would transmit under another name in order to keep the German sleuths from making a powerful effort to find her.

If this seemed specious, that was because it was specious. Mathilde did not reason very well much of the time. She thought she did; in fact Mathilde considered herself an individual of considerable aptitude and intelligence. The point was, that where it did not really matter, people had been indulging Mathilde most of her life. Bleicher indulged her in this. The most important aspect of his scheme was that it should succeed. As long as F-Section of S.O.E. understood that it was Mathilde sending them information, then Bleicher was quite content to indulge his mistress.

'The Cat' became 'Victoire', and the initial contact with London was made in late November, 1941. The British were duped, nor was there any reason for them not to be. Mathilde knew the call schedules, the call letters, all the prearranged security checks, the contexts and codes. She resumed transmitting exactly as she had done most of the preceding year.

Her first messages were as precisely routine as most of Inter-Allied's messages had been. They dealt with routine intelligence such as troop movements, new German defence installations, ships arriving and departing, most of it not quite true – obviously; the *Abwehr* certainly did not want to call in R.A.F. strikes against its own people – some of it was entirely true, but none of it critical nor very spectacular. It was Bleicher's idea to resume the contact with London without fanfare of any kind. Everything must appear essentially as it had been between the Cat, now 'Victoire', and F-Section of S.O.E.

For the Germans, but especially for Hugo Bleicher and Mathilde Carré, the wait until those first messages had been received, de-coded, acknowledged, and believed, was agonizing. They had only won a reluctant approval from Colonel Reile. If the scheme failed at this juncture, after so much effort and expense had been put into it, there would be harsh recrimination, no doubt about that.

London's response was gratifying, but as anyone knew whose contact with the British had been at all extensive, those people were masters at ever-so-politely saying one thing, and meaning another.

The exchanges continued, 'Marcel' transmitting, London receiving and acknowledging. For Mathilde, Renée Borni, and Henry Tabet – 'Marcel' – as well as for Bleicher, Captain Borchers, Dr Kaiser, and the German non-commissioned officers – all the complement of the Cattery – there remained an anxious doubt. They could not force the issue; it could only be resolved from the other end.

Finally, London put all their fears to rest. When preparations were in progress for the Allied raid on St Nazaire (which was to take place in the summer of 1942) London forwarded an urgent request for all available information respecting German defences at the great seaport, to be transmitted at once.

There was a two-fold backlash from this: one, obviously, was the clear implication that London was entirely satisfied Mathilde's renewed transmissions were genuine. The other, was that as soon as the *Abwehr* received this urgent request, it became a matter for speculation that the British might be contemplating a raid on the St Nazaire harbour, locks, and German ship-repair installations.

Finally, now, Mathilde and Hugo Bleicher could exult. The scheme was working. From the Cattery went forth a steady flow of information. It was not difficult to create acceptable fabrications. German troop movements could be factually reported without much danger of air strikes actually causing damage; the reports were based on the location of trains and convoys a day or two prior to broadcasting. Total fabrications were hazardous; Mathilde's messages were not the only ones being beamed to London. It would only take one set of messages reporting completely opposite bits of intelligence for the British to to realize that someone, either Mathilde or some other transmitter, was not telling the truth.

Dr Kaiser, the peace-time lawyer of Mannheim, supervised most of the messages Mathilde wrote, and as the British requests for more and more information came through, he was pressed for the kind of information it would be unsafe to send.

Bleicher's original idea had been to get as much information from the British as he gave them. He knew very well that S.O.E. had been air-dropping supplies, funds, and secret agents into France. He was also quite aware that Colonel Reile was not going to be satisfied with having Bleicher play cat-and-mouse with London, for any indefinite period of time. He and Mathilde conferred. She suggested that they ask London for money, and accordingly the request was forwarded, explaining that 'Victoire' required funds to meet expenses, as well as to pay her agents.

In due course the response came back to the effect that if Mathilde would visit the concierge of a particular house in Paris, she would receive funds. Mathilde and Bleicher drove into Paris the following day. Mathilde contacted the concierge and was given a packet of money amounting to 50,000 francs, not a fortune at all, but as Bleicher observed, the money was of secondary importance; the foremost factor was this additional evidence of British trust. And too, there was the concierge; now the *Abwehr* knew where to establish a fresh surveillance, with the expectation of gathering in members of the *Résistance*, and perhaps even British secret agents. And finally, there was now something substantial to show Colonel Reile.

Bleicher's concern with air-dropped Allied agents was justified. By the end of 1941 and over into the early months of 1942, Allied Intelligence had perfected techniques not only for parachuting agents into Occupied France, but of also air-dropping tons of demolition devices, weapons, radio equipment, and even large sums of money. They had also perfected a quite successful method of actually landing light aircraft – Lysanders – and picking up agents, as well as important Frenchmen, practically under the noses of Germans, and flying them to safety in England, usually at night.

The secret war, in fact, was becoming more than simply a source of annoyance to the Germans by the last months of 1941. France was being rather thoroughly infiltrated; S.O.E. agents of F-section were arriving with radio operators and radios almost at will. Not all eluded capture at landing, and many others did not enjoy their liberty very long after becoming established. The rate of failure was high. So was the mortality rate, but enough managed to drop from sight and surface later among the secret cells, to provide London with a stream of information. In time, of course, almost any of these genuine agents would have surpassed Mathilde in their value to London, but in late 1941 that was not Bleicher's foremost worry. What worried him more, as Christmas drew near, was that London might begin to suspect that the un-spectacular information arriving from 'Victoire' was noticeably in contrast to the more lurid and revelatory intelligence which had formerly reached London over her former signature, as the Cat.

But Hugo Bleicher was an exceptionally astute German. The Cattery was important to him. More important, it can be assumed, than promotion. It had been his idea, and it could be expected that he would do whatever had to be done to keep it functioning, and functioning successfully. The cost of failure for Germans in uniform in 1941 and 1942 was transfer to the frigid Russian front, at that time, late in the year, 1941, centred around Leningrad, where the 900-day siege was becoming a nightmare of unprecedented horror for the combatants of both sides, as well as for the civilians caught inside the utterly devasted city.

Bleicher's position was uncomfortable. He needed some kind of spectacular information to send London, something which would not only deceive the British, but something which would rebound creditably for the *Abwehr*.

Mathilde, among others at the Cattery, had a low regard of British canniness, but Hugo Bleicher, who disliked the British, especially the English, never made the common German mistake of under-rating his enemy. He knew that he was figuratively balancing on a swordblade. If he could come up with something spectacular he would be able to prolong the life of his false *réseau*. If he could not come up with something spectacular, then, obviously, the days of the Cattery were limited. Finally, assuming his deception could not survive indefinitely, then it must, as a last resort, strike one solid blow for Germany.

There was also the matter of verification. The British did not rush headlong into things. Whatever was transmitted to London through 'Victoire', had to be adequately valid to withstand London's scrutiny.

The upshot of all this came about in a way Hugo Bleicher did not expect, and his, as well as Mathilde Carré's part in it, subsequently put considerable strain on 'Victoire's' *réseau*. Their reasoning was sound, and like most of the triumphs in this war, or any other war, the revelation of what now occurred went back a year or more, and although it infringed upon a great many lives, none knew, in late 1941 or early 1942, that this was to be the case. As for Mathilde, her war, first as an agent of the Allies, and subsequently as a double agent for the Axis, had been largely confined to the land; to armies, air forces, land boundaries and land engagements. She was now to become involved with the sea, and with the sea-might of the adversary powers. Not directly, but with sufficient influence to tip the scales in a way which caused consternation throughout the free world.

The German navy, usually lost sight of in any consideration of the war's early days, when Hitler's *Wehrmacht* and *Luftwaffe* captured all attention with their matchless co-operation and invincible thrust, played a stellar role in the Norwegian campaign, which began in early April of 1940, and ended that same month. This was the only German operation of the war in which the navy played a leading role, and with good reason; it took a terrible beating.

The assault on Norway was planned so that the country's major seaports would be captured before a British expeditionary force could intervene, and accordingly Bergen, Trondheim, Narvik, Oslo, and Christiansand were besieged and blockaded by the German Navy.

Narvik, Christiansand, Bergen and Trondheim were all taken by noon of the same day, 9th April 1940. Warships blockaded them while the *Wehrmacht* drove overland. Oslo held out for an additional ten days, then capitulated. This was, in essence, the Norwegian campaign.

But swift as it was, Norway's surrender and occupation did not come as a cheap victory. Britain's Royal Navy, alerted to the imminence of the invasion, already had elements of its powerful fleet steaming through the North Sea. Admiral Whitworth, aboard the battleship *Warspite*, accompanied by nine destroyers, and an aircraft umbrella from the distant carrier, *Furious*, despite terrible weather, high seas, squall-rain, low visibility, entered Narvik Harbour and engaged the Germans in a deafening battle, sank a submarine, caught a German destroyer waiting to launch torpedoes from ambush, despatched her, then, at 1.30 p.m. came face to face with five German destroyers, and in one of the most savage sea engagements of the war, destroyed all five Germans, and in the ensuing chase, caught and sank three more German ships. The loss of eight of her capital warships in one prolonged engagement was something the German Navy could not afford. But these were not the only German sea-going casualties. Four more destroyers were caught in a fiord by dive-bombers, and bombed out of commission.* It was the worst naval disaster the Germans were to suffer in the Second World War to their surface fleet. Out of twenty destroyers, the Germans lost ten. Out of eight cruisers, they lost three. Three German warships which were heavily damaged but not sunk, were the pocket battleship *Lützow* and the cruisers *Scharnhorst* and *Gneisenau*.

Losses to the Royal Navy were not negligible, but neither were they as crippling as the German losses. Britain, still master of the seas, and desperately engaged in protecting a highly vulnerable Atlantic lifeline, was determined to destroy the German navy, and toward that goal exerted every effort to remain aware of the location of Germany's warships. The *Scharnhorst* and *Gneisenau*, which were eventually made sea-worthy after the Norwegian campaign, cruised the North Atlantic, often in consort, and in one two-month period sank or captured twenty-two Allied vessels. These vessels and the under-sea wolf packs contributed to an appalling fatality among Allied ships. Then, in early 1941, the *Scharnhorst, Gneisenau*, and another cruiser, the *Prinz Eugen*, were located in the French harbour of Brest, where the Royal Navy promptly set up a blockade, which was to last for about a year.

Germany's efforts to get her three warships out of the harbour at Brest and back to the sea-war, were unending, but cautious. It would have been pointless to order the cruisers to sea, with Britain's warships beyond the harbour, lying in wait. On the other side, the British were equally determined either to prevent the cruisers from leaving port, or, if they made the attempt, to sink them. But the British could not risk a close naval surveillance either; their navy was badly needed elsewhere, also, British warships off the coast of France were vulnerable to German air attacks. It was therefore decided to destroy the German warships from the air.

Britain's Air Force made a series of air attacks, but failed to damage any of the German vessels seriously. Meanwhile, orders were sent forth for the French espionage networks to concentrate on the harbour at Brest, and to let London know at the first indication that the Germans were preparing to make a dash for open water. Accordingly, one of the most outstanding Frenchmen of the *Résistance*, Gilbert Renault – code-named 'Colonel Remy' – who established the highly successful networks, *Confrérie de Notre Dame*, and *Centurie*, with cells from the mouth of the Loire to Brest, St Malo, Cherbourg, Caen, and the Seine estuary, forty *réseaux* in all, and who knew the Channel coast as well as anyone, undertook the surveillance for London. Henceforth, the German warships were under intense and round-the-clock observation.

The Germans decided in early 1942 that the ships must break out. The Battle of the Atlantic was nearing its apex. Orders were sent forth for the ships to steam out of the harbour at night, which would enable them to be clear of the straits by daybreak and, hopefully, clear of the Channel before the Royal Navy knew they were making for the open sea.

Gilbert Renault kept London appraised of everything the Germans did. There was no deception the Germans undertook to induce watchers to believe the ships were harbour-bound, that Renault did not correctly evaluate and report.

At this same time orders were received at the Cattery also to furnish London with information concerning the status of the *Scharnhorst*, and *Gneisenau*, and the *Prinz Eugen*. And it was done, but a totally different kind of information went out. London was assured that the three warships had been badly damaged by the R.A.F. bombing attacks. It was reported that although repairs were going forward, all three vessels could not possibly be made seaworthy short of several months.

These reports did not necessarily conflict. Renault was of the opinion that the ships would soon sail. Mathilde's messages, under her new code-name of 'Victoire', stated that the ships had been damaged, and while they would eventually be able to sail, it would not be for some time. In London, the general consensus was that, sooner or later, the ships would try to break out of their harbour, but probably not very soon.

Mathilde's messages had influence in London, since they were supposedly transmitted by the woman who had, in conjunction with Armand and Inter-Allied, provided the Allies with such a wealth of completely reliable information throughout most of the previous year – 1941.

In the first week of February, 1942, Renault sent the following message to London: "*Scharnhorst* and *Gneisenau* in condition for action. Departure probably to take place about eleven one evening or midnight during period of the next moon."

A week passed and the warships were still idle at their berths. The Cattery continued to send assurances to London that repair work was underway. On 7th February, Renault radioed that "Departure absolutely imminent....". For the next few days nothing happened, and the Cattery continued to send assurances that the ships were still unable to go to sea.

Renault had been 'crying fox' for several months, and the German warships were still at berth, Mathilde's messages had been less strident, more in keeping with what aerial observation showed, which was, simply, that the ships were still rigged against torpedo assaults in the harbour, obviously not cleared for sailing.

Then it happened. Winston Churchill had said that, in view of the situation in the Baltic, where the Royal Navy was to establish an invincible sea blockade, that the German warships at Brest would not attempt a break-out. "We do not think it likely . . . that these two vessels will be employed", he said.

The night of 11th February, with a Royal Navy Coastal Command patrol maintaining vigil – its radar equipment not functioning properly – the German warships broke out of Brest Harbour, racing for the open sea.

In the Germans' favour, the Royal Air Force did not make its customary overhead sweep after daybreak, the Germans reached the open sea, and London did not know until the following day that they had escaped.

12

'Victoire' The Huntress

The escape of Germany's three heavy cruisers, after a year's blockade and despite all the French espionage networks had done to render such a flight impossible, had immediate and far-reaching repercussions.

In Germany, of course, there was elation. Not only had the warships eluded the Royal Navy, but they had also eluded the Royal Air Force. Finally, Germany triumphantly announced that the ships had reached their destination untouched, and could now resume preying upon Allied shipping.

In Britain – and even in America – the lamentations and recriminations were loud and long. Churchill was compelled by both public and Parliamentary indignation to establish a board of enquiry. The results of this official investigation, which were not publicized until the war had ended, indicated that the government had been taken quite by surprise. And of course this 'surprise' was not the result of Gilbert Renault's constant, almost frantic warnings, it had to arise from the lulled suspicions encouraged by the soothing, and placating messages from 'Victoire'.

The British retaliated. Not on the high seas against the *Scharnhorst*, *Gneisenau*, and the *Prinz Eugen*, because the Germans took steps to prevent this. They retaliated by launching that raid against the docks at St Nazaire, which they had been planning since late in the previous year, when their requests for information about the St Nazaire defences, had aroused German interest.

The attack was a success, despite long-standing suspicion among the Germans that it might be undertaken, and also despite losses of two-thirds of the commando force. The locks were blown up, which created a hardship for German shipping, since this port was the only one on the Atlantic coast which had adequate facilities for repairing Germany's largest warships. Another commando raid near Le Havre, at Bruneval, was also a success. The raiders were able to destroy a German radar facility, and take away with them some radar equipment, which British scientists wished to evaluate.

But of course these, and other similar commando raids did not mitigate what had occurred at Brest. The indignation continued unabated, and meanwhile, at the Cattery, Hugo Bleicher and his mistress had to try and devise a way to ascertain if their part in the escape of the *Scharnhorst*, the *Gneisenau*, and the *Prinz Eugen* had hopelessly compromised them with London.

There was also a slight internal matter which required attention, Captain Borchers, who had always been a hard-drinking man, had become something of a liability. Because his work interfered with his drinking, he did less and less of the former while doing more and more of the latter. He was eventually replaced by Major Eschig, who had been serving in somewhat of a liaison capacity, his regular duty-station being the Harry Bauer villa, called *Abwehr* St Germain.

Another of the Cattery's internal difficulties was not as amenable to a tidy solution. Mathilde and Renée Borni were as implacable in their detestation of one another as ever. It did not make for exactly the atmosphere of a 'home away from home' that Hugo Bleicher had originally had in mind when he had advocated the establishment of the separate facility. Still, with the alternatives being Leningrad or Moscow, this constant friction was endurable and, in both cases, Bleicher's concern subsequent to the Brest debacle, whether Britain's trust had been forfeited or not, took precedence.

At roughly the same time, Mathilde demonstrated her scorn of double agents, with that unique capacity she possessed for making all judgments condemnatory against those who did the same things she did, while finding her own, identical actions, reasonable and even heroic.

Renée Borni told Hugo Bleicher that the Inter-Allied network had been in contact with a Frenchman René knew only by his code-name of 'Yolo'. He was, according to Renée, a double agent; the Germans of the Hotel Majestic, where a special section for the occupational internal services was housed, had relied heavily upon the collaboration of this prominent and rich French businessman, who had been, according to Renée, actually a member of Inter-Allied. He had never been caught, and Renée implied to Bleicher, for obvious reasons, that Mathilde, who knew this man well, had been protecting him.

Bleicher confronted Mathilde at once. She admitted knowing Yolo, but scoffed at the allegation that she had been protecting him, and in fact offered to take Bleicher to the double agent's business address. Bleicher naturally agreed, and Mathilde telephoned Yolo to make an appointment. The Frenchman was elated to hear from Mathilde and agreed to meet her, and meanwhile Bleicher verified from the special services office at the Hotel Majestic that the Germans there had put great store in what their collaborationist told them.

Bleicher was not prepared to rush in, gun drawn, as he had done with lesser people, and arrest a man in whom other Germans, and high-ranking ones at that, placed great confidence. He and Erich Borchers devised a plan to procure irrefutable proof that Yolo was a double agent. Mathilde was to appear at the Frenchman's office with a bandaged right hand, which she did, and during the course of their conversation, when Yolo gave her some information to be transmitted to London, Mathilde, exhibiting the bandaged hand, which made it impossible for her to write, asked Yolo to write it down for her, which the completely unsuspecting Frenchman did.

Mathilde then departed, met Bleicher outside, and handed him the hand-written, incriminating information. Bleicher at once went on to arrest Yolo, and Mathilde, with no desire to witness this affair, went to a nearby café to wait. Her subsequent comment was: "Well, Yolo had given them proofs of an excellent collaboration. He had played with both sides and that was too much. Now he was finished."

Also, at about this time, the Frenchman who had contacted Maitre Michel Brault some time earlier, after the destruction of his embryonic *réseau*, and the capture of most of its members, Pierre de Vomécourt, was still desperately seeking a way to make radio contact with S.O.E. in London, which had sent him to France by air-drop on 10th May 1941.

Maitre Brault had told de Vomécourt – whose code-name was Lucas – of Mathilde, the Cat, and of course in the meanwhile Inter-Allied had ceased to exist, most of its people had dropped from sight, and Maitre Michel Brault, who had often thought this might one day occur, and who had been appalled at Armand's and Mathilde's lack of discretion, knew nothing of the German deception. He believed Mathilde was still serving the Allies, and in his stark innocence agreed to seek a meeting between de Vomécourt and Mathilde.

As a result of what followed, and also because Pierre de Vomécourt, who miraculously survived the war, was a very noteworthy man who would play an important part in Mathilde's future, he deserves, as did Hugo Bleicher, more than a passing introduction.

Pierre de Vomécourt had been a captain in the French army at the time of the surrender. He came from an old and aristocratic family. The profession of arms was ingrained in the de Vomécourts. Pierre's grandfather had died under torture in the German-French conflict in 1870. Pierre's father had volunteered for service at the age of forty-five in the First World War, and had been killed in his first battle. Pierre's older brother, Jean, at school in England during the First World War, had lied about his age to get into the Royal Air Force. He was commissioned by the British when he was shot down and gravely wounded. Pierre's other brother, too young in 1918 by all standards, educated at Beaumont College, Old Windsor, eventually emerged with a British territorial commission.

All the de Vomécourts were courageous, cool men. Pierre went to England after the French capitulation, was trained for espionage, and was the first secret agent of S.O.E., French Section. Code-named 'Lucas', de Vomécourt was also the first S.O.E. agent to be parachuted into France, where, with his two brothers, Jean and Phillippe, along with several close and trusted friends including Henri Sevenet and the Marquis de Moustier, he undertook to organize a network, code-named 'Autogiro'.

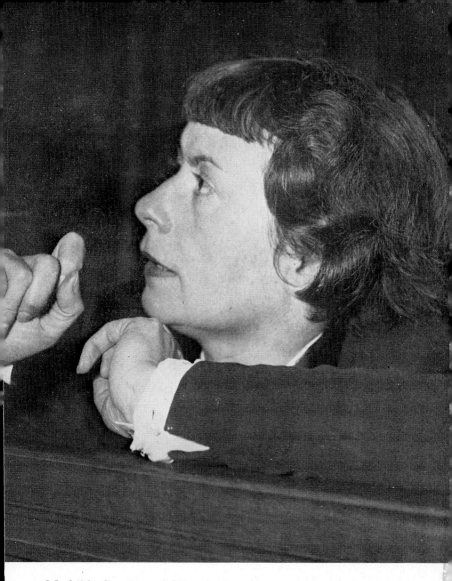

Mathilde Carré, aged forty, at the time of her trial in 1949

Hugo Bleicher, the member of the *Abwehr* with whom Mathilde Carré co-operated, in his tobacconist's shop near Lake Constance

Eventually de Vomécourt's network included Ben (Captain B.H.) Cowburn – code-named Benoit – a thirty-three-year-old mining engineer who had been born at Leigh in Lancashire, but who had resided in France, and about five other active agents, plus a number of French residents, including another nobleman, Comte Maurice du Puy, and a policitian, Octave Chantraine, mayor of Tendu.

Initially, de Vomécourt, a heavy-featured, dark-eyed man, did well; he, his brothers and Cowburn, the burly Lancashireman, were able to establish a number of cells, then the Vichy police arrested several of the group, and one by one they were almost all tracked down and captured. One man, André Bloch, the radioman, was put to torture by the Germans, and when he still refused to co-operate, he was shot to death. With the loss of Bloch, what remained of de Vomécourt's shattered network was unable to contact London, which was where Maitre Brault, contacted by de Vomécourt, set up the meeting between de Vomécourt and Mathilde.

It appeared that de Vomécourt's intention was to report to London what disasters had befallen his network, and to request funds which would enable him to start over again, along with additional air-dropped S.O.E. agents, and a very badly needed radioman – a "musician" – to replace the heroic and unfortunate André Bloch. But de Vomécourt was a careful man. He knew from sad experience that French collaborators as well as zealous German counter-intelligence agents were everywhere. For these reasons he was wary when Maitre Brault suggested the meeting with Mathilde. But, as so often happened at that time, the alternatives were limited to a choice of two: do nothing, and do it desperately, or run a risk, and confer with this woman Maitre Brault said was in radio contact with London. De Vomécourt chose the only real course open to him. Maitre Brault contacted Mathilde, and arranged for the meeting to take place at the Café Georges V, on the Champs Elysees.

As a matter of fact the *Abwehr* knew of Maitre Brault's connection with Inter-Allied, but he was, like a few others, considered more valuable free than imprisoned. The German

view was that a man such as Maitre Brault, would eventually
provide them with more secret agents. And how right they
were!

At this first meeting Maitre Brault introduced de
Vomécourt as Monsieur Lucas. Mathilde was delighted. So
was Hugo Bleicher, sitting quietly at a nearby table enjoying
an aperitif and a French newspaper.

Monsieur Lucas was prepared to trust the stocky,
curvaceous woman with the dark green eyes and glistening
dark hair, because, obviously, Maitre Brault trusted her – and
also because he really had no second choice. He told Mathilde
that he was a British agent, and asked if she could transmit
several messages to London for him.

Mathilde liked de Vomécourt, which may not have been
actually much of a commendation; Mathilde liked many men.
They were nearly the same age; Mathilde was thirty-one in
1941, Piere de Vomécourt was thirty-five. He was not
handsome, but he was charming, and Mathilde had always
succumbed easily to masculine charm. She told de Vomécourt
she would take his request under consideration, and would
meet him again. Thus ended de Vomécourt's first contact with
the woman he would remember as long as he lived.

Mathilde reported the full conversation to Bleicher, who
was delighted to have the opportunity to apprehend
additional enemy agents even though there were some
involvements, both external and internal, which posed
problems. He therefore told Mathilde to arrange a second
meeting with Monsieur Lucas – they knew him by no other
name at this time – and assure him that she would transmit
messages for him.

All this occurred roughly a month or five weeks before the
Brest episode involving the three German warships. De
Vomécourt initially met Mathilde late in December of 1941, at
about the time instructions were filtering down from the
Cattery to begin answering London's enquiries about the
warships in a manner designed to allay British suspicion. On
this score, both Bleicher and Mathilde were sufficiently
occupied, without any fresh involvements. But above all else,
Hugo Bleicher desired to maintain the Cattery as a successful

counter-Intelligence facility. He was reasonably certain by this time that London suspected nothing. He and Mathilde, both, were also aware, perhaps she more than he, that unless the Cattery continued to produce in a worthwhile fashion, the *Abwehr* would close it down.

This would have been a set-back for Sergeant Bleicher, but for Mathilde, it could be fatal. If the Germans no longer needed her, she could very easily end up at Mathausen or Buchenwald.

Another worry for Bleicher, and he frequently alluded to it in his conversations with Mathilde, had to do with the possibility that his voluptuous, green-eyed paramour might again defect, might become a triple agent. In allowing Mathilde to meet Monsieur Lucas alone, Bleicher was running the risk of having her betray the *Abwehr*, exactly as she had betrayed Inter-Allied, and, while professing continued loyalty to the Germans, begin functioning again for the Allies.

There were things to be said in favour of the Eastern front. Not many, obviously, but in Russia, a German soldier would not be at the mercy of a French woman.

For Mathilde, the game was the same, but with new pawns, which was commendable, since the Germans were now only apprehending a few informers, here and there, and an occasional courier. Inter-Allied was dead. True, a few people such as Maitre Brault, had been left free, under surveillance, as bait, but without an access to the Tudor network, or some of the other large networks. *Abwehr* successes were not as spectacular as they had been.

If she could induce London, through Monsieur Lucas, to send over supplies, funds, but most desirable of all, secret agents, her future would be assured.

But Mathilde was also conscious of the possibilities which troubled Hugo Bleicher. She had worked out a creditable defence of her actions, during her months with the Germans, if she were ever called upon to justify all that she had done. She was a woman who understood men. But these were thoughts to keep in reserve, and when she went to her next meeting with Monsieur Lucas, what followed made it abundantly clear that she was not, at that time, thinking of anything but serving the *Abwehr*.

She and Monsieur Lucas met the second time in a cubby-hole office he had rented in the heart of Paris, and Mathilde told him she would transmit messages to London for him. They had a rather lengthy, pleasant talk. Mathilde told Monsieur Lucas the same story she had told London, that after Armand had been caught by the Germans, she had carried on. Lucas, for his part, was fairly open and trusting, not entirely, however, for while he gradually came to trust Mathilde, both his training and his recent disasters in the field of espionage, had made Pierre de Vomécourt a very guarded man. He did, however, express a hope that they could work together in creating a new network.

When Mathilde returned to the Cattery, she and Hugo Bleicher had a long conference. Mathilde said that, in order to cultivate Lucas, and establish a close working relationship with him, in which he would come to freely contact her, she obviously could not continue to operate at the Cattery. What she proposed was that she be allowed to find an apartment in Paris, move in, and live alone.

Bleicher's msigivings must have returned. On the other hand Mathilde's argument was valid. If they were now going to bait Allied agents into a trap, using Lucas, he must not be allowed even the faintest suspicion.

Mathilde was allowed to select a flat at 26 rue de la Faisanderie, in an excellent neighbourhood, and move in. But Bleicher moved in with her. Protests were useless. They became Monsieur and Madame Jean Castel. He was to be introduced as her husband, a Belgian; this was to account for Bleicher's accented French. They worked out a credible 'cover'; Bleicher as the Belgian, Jean Castel, was a sympathiser with the French *Résistance*. He helped his wife in her secret work against the Germans.

Eventually, when the new friendship between Monsieur Lucas and Mathilde made a visit by Lucas to the apartment at 26 rue de la Faisanderie, necessary, Mathilde introduced Lucas to 'Jean Castel'. At this meeting Lucas asked Mathilde to send a message for him to London, asking that F-section

S.O.E., acknowledge receipt, and agree that future messages be sent through 'Victoire'.

London, elated to learn that Lucas was not in German hands, quickly responded; Lucas was to use 'Victoire's' wave length. He was also to report what had happened to him since his last communication, months earlier. But elation in London was tempered with caution. Lucas, like other secret agents, had specific words and terms known only to him, and his superiors in London. He was duly queried by London on these points, and because it was indeed Lucas at the other end, in France, he confirmed his identity to London's satisfaction.

Lucas's two most important messages, over the 'Victoire' transmitter – now re-located from the Cattery to a house in Neuilly – asked for an air-dropped radioman to replace André Bloch, and for funds.

London's reply to the request for a radioman, was to the effect that none were immediately available. The answer to Lucas's request for funds was more gratifying. He was directed to contact a foreign diplomat at Vichy, which he did – under close German surveillance – and was handed a large amount of money.

For Mathilde and Hugo Bleicher, the procrastination over sending a radioman was a disappointment. But when the *Abwehr* was able to add a supposedly neutral foreign diplomat to its list of alien enemies, the earlier disappointment was cancelled out.

For Pierre de Vomécourt, the prompt arrival of the funds was proof that Mathilde was exactly what she had claimed to be.

13

Monsieur Lucas

Pierre de Vomécourt had a rendezvous with Ben Cowburn – code-named 'Benoit', but called "Benny" by de Vomécourt – and another agent, a close associate of happier days, Roger Cottin. Cottin, born in France of English parents, was a large, powerful man, called by the others *"Roger les Cheveux blancs"* because of his mane of prematurely white hair.

Cowburn and Cottin were impressed by the money de Vomécourt showed them. All three had been living very frugally since radio contact with London had been disrupted. They were even more jubilant at de Vomécourt's announcement that he and Mathilde Carré had agreed to work together. It would now be possible, with just a little luck, to create another network.

To celebrate, the three British agents proposed to have dinner at an elegant restaurant, and the gallant thing to do, of course, was invite Mathilde to join them, which they did, and the evening passed very pleasantly, even exuberantly, under the observation of several plainclothes *Abwehr* men.

The association between 'Madame Castel' and 'Monsieur Lucas' seemed destined to prosper. Lucas asked London for a supply of air-dropped weapons to be used in arming members of a new network and London obligingly replied that the supplies would be delivered at night by the Royal Air Force, air-dropped into a field not far from Le Mans. This air-drop was to be made on a bitterly cold January night. When Mathilde returned from the dinner party with this information, Bleicher was not just pleased, he was enthusiastic. He and Mathilde devised a plan whereby Bleicher, as the Belgian sympathiser 'Jean Castel', would offer his car and driver to Monsieur Lucas for the trip to the countryside beyond Le Mans, the night of the air-drop.

Bleicher, as 'Jean Castel', would volunteer to go along and offer his help.

Mathilde gave this information to Monsieur Lucas, who sent Roger Cottin on ahead to locate the field where the arms and ammunition were to be dropped. There, in a small village, Roger contacted a local *résistant*, a schoolteacher named Bernier, who was a member of a Le Mans *maquis* group, and completed plans for the drop.

Finally, on the night the episode was to take place, Mathilde and 'Jean Castel' met Monsieur Lucas at a café, at about five o'clock, and here Monsieur Lucas met the chauffeur who was to drive them all to Le Mans. He was introduced as another Belgian sympathiser, Monsieur Severin. He was also a non-commissioned officer of the *Abwehr*.

They drove south-west from Paris to the Sarthe, through the bitterly cold night, found Roger waiting at a pre-arranged spot, with the schoolteacher, and resumed their way to the field in the car, which was now rather crowded.

Neither Monsieur Lucas nor Jean Castel said much, and from Le Mans to the designated field beyond the hamlet of Vaas, there was even less conversation.

When the field was reached, there was little to do but wait. They stamped around to keep warm, listened for an aircraft, and watched the brittle, empty, winter night sky. Jean Castel had brought along some sandwiches, and hot coffee in a thermos flask. It was a long, and increasingly dismal wait. No aircraft arrived.

Shortly before dawn, long after the drop was to have been made, they piled stiffly back into the car and drove to a farmhouse, where they got warm, and finally, at daybreak, frustrated, half-frozen, and angry, drove back to Paris.

For Mathilde the disappointment was tinged with worry; if the British had by now become suspicious, she would be in genuine peril. For Bleicher, who had spent a very uncomfortable night in vain, there was reason to be upset and irritable.

Monsieur Lucas had two reactions to the abortive night-long episode. One, understandably, was disappointment and annoyance. He asked Mathilde to send off an enquiry, and in

due course an answer was received: Bad weather had
grounded the aircraft in England. His other reaction was a
very faint suspicion. All that long night in the field with the
two 'Belgians', Castel and Severin, there had been a sense of
something other than anticipation.

For the time being he decided to be very careful. Also, not
long before, a friend and close associate of Maitre Brault, a
man who had helped the defunct Inter-Allied organization in
its early days, Armand de Dampierre, had been picked up by
the Germans. Maitre Brault was at a loss; de Dampierre had
not been a regular informer, and yet, obviously, someone who
had known of his earlier contact, had informed against him. It
could have been any of the former members of Inter-Allied,
but if this were so, why had the Germans waited so long to
make the arrest?

But there were always mitigating circumstances, especially
in war. For Pierre de Vomécourt, always more or less existing
in the limbo of secret agents the world over, the doubts always
had to exist side by side with the hopes. It was desirable to
anticipate trouble; it was just rarely possible to do so. Then,
Mathilde received a message for him from F-Section, and the
manner in which he received the message reinforced his
suspicions.

This message was received by the station at Neuilly, which
was no great distance from the heart of Paris, being just north
of the Bois de Boulogne, on the Seine, and yet when Mathilde
delivered the message to Lucas it had been lying somewhere,
obviously, being held in abeyance, for many hours.

The substance of the message was that F-Section would
have a light aircraft, a Lysander, pick Lucas up at a field near
Chartres that same night. Mathilde handed him the message
just past three o'clock that afternoon, although it had been
received at Neuilly the previous day.

Chartres being fifty miles south-west of Paris, and public
transportation being entirely unsatisfactory, there was no way
for Lucas to reach Chartres, let alone the field beyond the
ancient town where the Lysander would land, in time to keep
the appointment. Explanations concerning the delay in
delivering the message were of course forthcoming. Mathilde

had never been unable to come up with alibis, but perhaps inevitably, Lucas began to worry, and to wonder.

The real reason the message had been held up, was because Mathilde and Hugo Bleicher had no intention, at this time, of allowing Monsieur Lucas, or any other British secret agent, to escape from the Continent. On the other hand, there was the worry about what must follow if he were *not* allowed to go. London would at once suspect that Lucas was in German hands, and since he had been working closely with Mathilde, she was bound to come under suspicion. She had been involved in several episodes of late, which, if added to, would certainly create doubts.

While Bleicher and Mathilde were pondering, the Lysander arrived, and departed, and London wondered why Lucas had not been at the field to meet it. But that was not Lucas's latest worry, nor was it Bleicher's or Mathilde's latest worry. Bleicher had finally made a bad mistake. He arrested a Frenchman from Vichy named Michel: Colonel Francois Michel, an officer who had been aiding the *Résistance* for some time, and was authorized to travel across Occupied France. His passport had a rather distinctive photograph of him attached to it. Colonel Michel's friends and underground associates had all, at one time or another seen this excellent picture.

Colonel Michel was another of Maitre Brault's friends and underground associates, and during the course of Hugo Bleicher's investigation of Maitre Brault, it had come to Bleicher's attention that Colonel Michel frequently had long, secret visits with the lawyer. It did not require very much investigating to turn up the fact that Colonel Michel had other, equally questionable contacts. Colonel Michel was, if not an actual participant in underground activities, then at least a helpful sympathiser, and since it had been Bleicher's purpose, from the very beginning, to use Maitre Brault as the bait by which other sympathisers could be caught, Hugo Bleicher had Colonel Michel arrested while he was on his way to visit the office of Maitre Brault.

He then sent Mathilde to the lawyer's office to verify that, in fact, it had indeed been Colonel Michel for whom the lawyer was waiting. When Maitre Brault told Mathilde that he expected an important and confidential visitor, she took from her purse the passport photograph Bleicher had provided her with, to guarantee the identity of Bleicher's prisoner, and, holding the picture, asked Maitre Brault if that was the man he was expecting. Maitre Brault confirmed that it was indeed the man, and Mathilde departed.

Several days passed before it was suddenly made clear to Maitre Brault that the photograph of the man who had failed to keep his appointment at the lawyer's office, was the identical photograph Colonel Michel had on his passport.

The implication was clear – and completely unnerving – Mathilde was a German agent. Colonel Michel had been apprehended by the Germans, with his passport, naturally, and there was only one way for anyone to have possession of the photograph from his passport: if it was given to them by the Germans.

For Maitre Brault, the elapsed time between Mathilde's last visit to his office, with Colonel Michel's photograph, and his dawning realization that she was a double agent, involved a full forty-eight hours. For the people who were involved in what now occurred, it was a very fateful forty-eight hours.

Perhaps Bleicher realized, finally, that he had blundered. Possibly he was ready, now, to apprehend the lawyer. In either case, even as Maitre Brault decided he had to find Lucas and warn him against Mathilde, Hugo Bleicher decided Maitre Brault should be arrested. Accordingly, he despatched a carload of *Abwehr* men to the lawyer's apartment, and what saved Maitre Brault was one of these eleventh-hour flukes that infrequently intervene.

Maitre Brault was with his wife at a theatre, that night. At his apartment his sister-in-law was at home. Before the play was finished, Maitre Brault left to go home. He arrived long after the concierge had retired, and entered the apartment unnoticed. His sister-in-law had also retired. No one knew Maitre Brault had entered the apartment.

He went to bed, and just before dawn was awakened by a series of loud noises at the front door. His sister-in-law arose to ascertain the reason for the disturbance, and when she called out, the answer came in loud and unmistakable tones, *"Police Allemande"*, followed by a demand to open the door.

Maitre Brault sprang from bed, ran outside to a neglected stairway, raced up it into an unused, musty little room just below the eaves, which in former times had been a maid's quarters, and hid.

Downstairs, the Germans spread to ransack and search the apartment. They questioned the sister-in-law, who had not known Maitre Brault had come home the night before, as well as Madame, who also said her husband had not returned to the flat. Maitre Brault's daughter, a girl of sixteen, who waited with her aunt, her mother, and the Germans, for Maitre Brault to come home, finally said she must leave, or be late for school, and the Germans allowed her to go.

While the Germans grimly waited, the young girl went to the nearest telephone, called several of her father's friends, told them what had happened, begged them to warn anyone the Germans might also be seeking, then went along to school. From this source the alarm went out, and, as Colonel Maurice Buckmaster of S.O.E.'s F-Section was to note in his book *They Fought Alone* written after the war, because the Germans had no friends in Occupied France, while the enemies of Germany, despite former differences, had to be friends, it was only a matter of hours before the news, and its clear implication of what had happened, was surreptitiously spread among, not only Maitre Brault's business associates, but also among his friends of the underground.

The Germans were still waiting at the apartment, hours later, when elsewhere the alarm was being given. They did not depart until shortly before noon. During that time Maitre Brault spent a very long and very uncomfortable six or seven hours in the attic, occasionally peeking down from the eaves to see if the *Abwehr* car was gone.

When the Germans finally left, Maitre Brault made his escape, with the aid of his family, and, against the strong possibility that the *Abwehr* had the building under surveillance, he used the rear areas and the changing light of late-day to accomplish his purpose.

It was the lawyer's intention to flee to Unoccupied France,

which was for the moment his only resource, but the Germans were, even this early, in 1942, considering the complete and total occupation of France, which they would not undertake for roughly another year, and were sufficiently influential in Vichy to demand the surrender of French subjects in the enclave. Maitre Brault's alternatives were nil, and he knew it. However, this courageous middle-aged man was not quite ready to abandon Paris. There was still one person who had to be warned, and since none of Maitre Brault's associates knew anything at all about 'Monsieur Lucas', it was entirely up to the lawyer to personally make the contact.

When the two men met, Maitre Brault, the man of logic and law, told Lucas all that he knew, but he would not say he could prove Mathilde Carré was the one who had betrayed him. All he could say as fact, was that she had had in her possession, Colonel Michel's passport photograph, and that the raid on his apartment by the *Abwehr* was coincidental to her last visit to his office, with the photograph.

Lucas was not a lawyer. He was a very astute secret agent in the most perilous situation of his career. It did not matter to him whether or not Mathilde was the traitor. At this point it mattered only that she might be – that someone was – and the best course for Lucas to follow, after his conversation with Maitre Brault, was to exercise extreme caution – which is what he did.

Meanwhile Maitre Brault made good his escape to Vichy. There, he contacted a naval attaché at the United States Embassy, and gave him the information concerning recent events in Paris. He also made contact with the United States Intelligence organization in Switzerland, at that time headed by Allan Dulles, and sent them a second report. His final effort to warn London that the Germans had in all probability penetrated the 'Victoire' *réseau*, was through a British secret agent working through the Vichy French Intelligence Agency. Oddly enough, none of these messages reached London in time to prevent a very near thing for Pierre de Vomécourt – Monsieur Lucas.

Subsequent to the flight of Maitre Brault, Lucas met Mathilde, and told her of the lawyer's near-apprehension. She

responded by showing both consternation and sympathy. She
told Lucas that they should immediately concentrate on doing
everything which could be done to facilitate the lawyer's
escape from France.

She then made her own inadvertent blunder, exactly as
Bleicher had done. She offered to procure forged papers of
identity for Maitre Brault which would enable him to leave
the Continent.

On the face of it, since this was how all secret agents
travelled through Occupied France, this was not an unusual
offer. But Mathilde was dealing with a man who was almost
positive she was a traitor. If she was a good actress, Monsieur
Lucas must have been an even better actor. He went along
with her suggestion, and she went at once to Hugo Bleicher
with the proposal that the papers be issued. Bleicher agreed.
Whether he did so because he really no longer cared whether
Maitre Brault escaped, or whether he agreed, with the plan in
mind to arrest the French lawyer while he was in transit, using
the false identity, only Hugo Bleicher knew, but in either case,
he got the papers, and Mathilde met again with Monsieur
Lucas, and gave him the documents.

This was all Lucas needed to be sure Mathilde was actually a
double agent. The documents were not forgeries; they were
genuine German letters of identification with all the correct
German stamps and signatures affixed.

Lucas took the papers, thanked Mathilde for them, made
an appointment with her for dinner, and departed. She of
course reported to Bleicher and went to get ready to keep her
dinner engagement.

Bleicher made another mistake, but this time perhaps it was
an understandable one. He did not have Mathilde followed,
when she went to keep her appointment with Lucas.

She had certainly proved herself a willing and trustworthy
collaborator of late, and she had been meeting Lucas
privately for more than a week. Bleicher's mistake was not
really a mistrust of Mathilde, anyway, it was his error of
judgment in assessing Monsieur Lucas. He assumed that
Mathilde, who could handle men so adeptly, could also
handle this man. Perhaps under different circumstances she

could have, but this time she was confronting a man who knew very well that his life was in danger. Even a very sensual, voluptuous woman's charms, were not enough under these circumstances.

Monsieur Lucas was waiting at the café when Mathilde arrived. He was, as always, an epitome of good manners and charm. They ordered dinner, had a good wine – as good a wine as it was possible to get in Paris during the German occupation – and for a while they simply enjoyed themselves and their surroundings. Pierre de Vomécourt was as much an accomplished intriguist, in his fashion, as Hugo Bleicher was in his.

14

A Match For Mathilde

For Mathilde the strain had existed since that bleak night at La Santé, and subsequently it had become worse. The sense of security she had briefly enjoyed at *Abwehr* St Germain before the move to the Cattery, had begun to wear thin shortly after the move. Regardless of Bleicher's assurances, she was very much aware of the trainloads of hapless people leaving Paris almost daily for the interior of Germany. It was common knowledge that to be sent to Germany was to be sent to one's death.

Furthermore, by now she was also aware that Hugo Bleicher, whether he hauled her bath water, as he had done many times, or whether he took her to dinner at the best cafés, or not, was fully capable of sending her into Germany without remorse.

There was something else she could not have escaped noticing. Allied resolve was not the same in 1941 as it had been in 1939, or even the previous year. The Germans had been unable to invade England; they were suffering terrible losses in Russia, and a slowly gathering momentum of attrition was wearing them down, even in *Festung Europa*. The French underground was even beginning to challenge them in open combat, with signs that this powerful undercurrent of armed resistance was going to continue and increase.

For her dinner companion, who was a shrewd, hard man of great resourcefulness, there were even fewer illusions. He had not staked his life on victory because he had thought it an improbability, and he did not intend to risk it now on the possibility that Mathilde was not a traitor. He very quietly asked Mathilde who, besides herself, could have betrayed Maitre Brault. When she hesitated, at first, to reply, he asked her who else could have betrayed Armand de Dampierre,

pointing out that all of Inter-Allied's leadership had long been
gone, and if any of them had done it, the Germans would have
arrested de Dampierre months ago.

Finally, he told her that the supposedly forged German
documents she had given him for Maitre Brault, were not
forgeries at all; they were genuine originals. How had she
managed to acquire these, unless she got them directly from
the Germans?

As for the passport photograph of Colonel Michel, there
was no possible way for her to have had it in her possession,
unless it was given to her by the Germans.

Mathilde could not talk her way out of this thicket of valid
accusations. She had been able to create reasonable alibis,
now and then, for an occasional single suspicion, but the weight
of evidence was too overwhelming this time.

In a highly emotional outburst, she told Monsieur Lucas
who Jean Castel was: Sergeant Hugo Bleicher of the *Abwehr*.
For a month Bleicher had been developing Monsieur Lucas as
a means for baiting Allied agents and supplies into France.
But it was always Bleicher; it was never Mathilde. She had
been Bleicher's pawn; she had never wanted to serve the
Germans. At least one thing she said was true; if Bleicher
discovered that she had confessed her real position to
Monsieur Lucas, he would have her executed.

She warned Lucas that everything he wirelessed to London
was used by the *Abwehr* against the Allies. But for Lucas the
problem was not as simple as that. He could of course, have
made an attempt to warn London, or he could have
transmitted only innocuous messages. His greater problem,
beside trying to save his life, and the lives of his friends,
Cowburn and Cottin, was how to extricate himself without
arousing Hugo Bleicher's suspicion, and that, very clearly,
would not be simple at all. One never had to like an enemy,
but only fools underrated them.

Lucas's decision was to continue the charade with
Mathilde. Perhaps, if Mathilde had told him how she had
supervised the apprehension of so many people, not as
Bleicher's unwilling captive, but as his willing consort, Lucas
might have reacted differently. All she told him about the

Pierre de Vomécourt with Attorney Mercier

Mathilde being questioned in the dock and (below) striking an attitude of resignation

earlier disintegration of Inter-Allied, was that the organization had been penetrated by German Intelligence. She did not tell him that she, alone, had made it possible for that penetration to be as deep and far-reaching as it was.

But even had Lucas known the full extent of Mathilde's perfidy, his own plight would not have been any different, and because he was a man of penetrating intelligence, he doubtless surmised as much of the basic truth as she had with-held from him.

Also, Lucas was in a position, after Mathilde's confession, which no other man excepting Bleicher had ever been in; he could have informed against her to the Germans – except that it would have been pointless, even if the Germans captured him. Throwing someone to the wolves accomplished little, if one were also in process of being thrown to them.

As for trust, Lucas had no real alternative; if he continued the association with Mathilde, he had to trust her. It was like trying to balance on the cutting edge of a very sharp sword. When she told Lucas that she wanted only to be revenged upon the Germans for forcing her to act as their pawn, Lucas had to accept that statement in good faith, while at the same time never sleeping in the same bed twice.

There was one fundamental reason for Lucas to believe Mathilde. The tide of the war was definitely beginning to turn against the Germans; in Russia, particularly, the war was not going well, and Russia was now an ally of the British. Mathilde, the adept tight-rope walker, would most certainly abandon the losing side, but in order to do this successfully, she would need friends on the winning side; she would need someone like Lucas who could later defend her to London.

Lucas may even have suspected what was certainly true of this uniquely self-centred, amoral Frenchwoman; she wanted to be the focus of favourable attention – the admired, desired, terribly clever secret agent. She would willingly become a triple agent, to save her life, of course, but also so that she might someday emerge as the most successful and glamorous secret agent of the war.

Mathilde Carré was certainly never a woman to be seriously involved with, but now and then, in the lives of most men, such a woman comes along, and for Pierre de Vomécourt she had come along at this most dangerous period of his life.

He thought about killing her, but obviously that would, without any question, put an end to everything, and there was a very faint possibility that he and his friends might emerge alive, otherwise. It was a very faint possibility, but it existed, and shooting Mathilde would utterly destroy even that tenuous chance. One result of killing Mathilde would be the destruction of Lucas's only access to a wireless transmitter. Alive, at least until she decided to betray him as she had all her former acquaintances, he could still send messages to London, and right now it was imperative that F-Section be warned against the 'Victoire' network.

So Mathilde lived, and by so doing was enabled to participate in one of the most unique adventures of a secret agent in the Second World War. But before that happened, Lucas had to devise a way to keep London from trustingly sending any more messages through the 'turned-around' facility at Neuilly, like the one concerning the abortive arms air-drop near Le Mans.

The only way to do this, was with Mathilde's help, so he told her that henceforth they would work together, and she must now become a triple agent. Mathilde agreed. Then Lucas proved his canniness. He told Mathilde, as a confidence, that there had recently been an impromptu meeting of secret agents and representatives of several underground groups, in Paris – which was true. In fact, both Lucas and Roger Cottin had attended. Also, it was almost a certainty that the Germans had known of this meeting, which meant that Bleicher, if he had not not already known of the meeting, could certainly verify it, which would be proof that Lucas's confidence in Mathilde was genuine.

Then, having planted his 'truth', Lucas planted his 'lie', which was nothing more or less than the basis for, among other things, all good propaganda. If people are sure something is true, they are then psychologically conditioned to believe what is said in conjunction with the truth, even though it is not true.

Having provided Mathilde with the truth, which she was to carry back to Hugo Bleicher, Lucas then provided the lie.

Mathilde was to tell Bleicher that the result of this clandestine meeting, was that in order for the various, and overlapping underground networks to have clearly defined areas of operations, it had been decided that someone would have to go to London, and, in conference with British Intelligence, help to create specific delineations and guidelines. The person who had been chosen for the trip to London, was Monsieur Lucas.

Mathilde must convince Bleicher that Lucas must be allowed to depart safely from France, so that when he returned, he would be able to give Mathilde information on future air-drops, the arrivals of additional secret agents, and, eventually, a list of the underground networks of France. It was to be a very tempting bait for Bleicher. Or, if Bleicher preferred, when Monsieur Lucas returned to France, Bleicher could wait until another top-level meeting of underground officials was convened by Lucas, for the dissemination of the information he would bring from London, and in one mass arrest apprehend all the leaders at one time. In either case, the triumph for Hugo Bleicher would be dazzling. He would have been able to prove by example that the *Abwehr*, as an Intelligence organization, was superior to its antagonistic rival, the Gestapo.

Lucas's *pièce de résistance* was this: he would try hard to convince British Intelligence that the best way to prevent friction among the French underground leaders, would be for the British to send back with Lucas an officer of general rank.

Not even the *Wehrmacht* had captured a British General in France. Hopefully, Lucas's bait would tantalize higher *Abwehr* officers than Sergeant Bleicher. Hopefully, too, it would appeal on the grounds that if the *Abwehr* accomplished such a coup, its long-time and bitter rival, the Gestapo, would be properly humiliated.

Nor had Lucas overlooked Bleicher; if a sparse-haired, middle-aged, myopic non-commissioned officer could actually be directly responsible for the capture of a British General Officer, at the same time he led a raid which would bag every important underground leader of the entire Paris area, without a doubt he would emerge from the war as the most productive counter-Intelligence officer of the German forces of occupation.

Mathilde had doubts about Bleicher or his superiors taking such bait. Lucas also had doubts, but he was committed, therefore he told Mathilde she must make the effort; must be a very convincing actress.

She returned from this meeting with Lucas to the Castel residence at 26 rue de la Faisanderie. Bleicher listened to all she had to report, and instead of being wary, he was delighted. As Lucas had anticipated, Bleicher recognized the dazzling possibilities. Of course he could not make any unilateral authorization. A scheme as bold as this required clearance through the office of Bleicher's commanding officer, Colonel Reile.

While Lucas, Ben Cowburn and Roger Cottin waited – half expecting to be betrayed by Mathilde, and arrested at any moment – they began organizing a local *réseau*, with the thought in mind that if they were apprehended by the Germans, there would be someone left behind to continue their espionage activities.

As for Hugo Bleicher, who had so often in the past left little doubt that he did not completely trust Mathilde, now he did trust her. In fact, when Colonel Reile, the wary sceptic, said something on this subject, Bleicher respectfully, but adamantly, rejected the notion of treachery. Mathilde had collaborated so whole-heartedly of late, Bleicher's trust seemed entirely justified.

There was another obstacle, however. The *Abwehr* was required to clear anything of this magnitude through the Gestapo, and obviously the Gestapo was unlikely to consider with favour anything which might rebound to the credit of the *Abwehr*. (Eventually, the *Abwehr* was absorbed by the Gestapo. Their antagonism was basically political. No particular failure caused the *Abwehr's* decline, but the kind of blunder Hugo Bleicher was shortly to be involved in, certainly hastened it.)

True to expectations, Paris headquarters of the Gestapo, when brought current on the Lucas affair, opposed allowing any British secret agent to leave France, regardless of the possibility of future successes. The Gestapo took the view that

Lucas, and anyone he was known to have contacted, should be immediately executed.

Colonel Reile, having approved Bleicher's scheme, would not yield, so, in the end, the Gestapo assented. When this news reached Bleicher, he at once instructed Mathilde to meet Lucas and confirm that the Germans had agreed to his departure and return.

Lucas, under great stress during the interim, contacted his brother, who resided in the unoccupied segment of France, and when they met in Paris, Lucas explained his situation in detail and requested that his brother return to Vichy and send warnings to London, in case something happened which would prevent Lucas from getting out of France. This was done. Lucas's brother sent the warning.

Finally, Mathilde visited Lucas with the news that the Germans were agreeable to his departure. They particularly wanted him to bring back the General. They also hoped he would return with a list of the names of British secret agents in France. They assumed he would do this, as a leader of British espionage in France. The only reluctance, she reported, was on the part of the Gestapo, which had assented only because Colonel Reile would not budge, but with the Gestapo also involved, the danger for Lucas had more than doubled. Excluding the deaths-head men of the SS there was no segment of the German armed forces as brutal and deadly as the notorious *Geheime Staatspolizei*, the Gestapo.

The *Abwehr* was an Intelligence organization. The Gestapo, established in 1933 by Herman Göring, had always been a political police force. It had never been concerned with Intelligence and had never employed the subterfuges of an Intelligence organization. Counter-Intelligence, detection or prevention, the *Abwehr* basics, were not the Gestapo's primary objective since its founding had been the elimination of all dissent, in Germany before the war, and in the wake of Germany's conquering armies, afterwards. It was therefore understandable that when it was called into conference in the Lucas affair, both politically and traditionally, it was conditioned to oppose the *Abwehr's* deviousness. The Gestapo's unfailing reaction to any and all dissent was either a bullet in the back of the neck on the spot, or deportation to one of its death camps.

Lucas had reason to feel increasingly imperilled. As he sat with Mathilde in the small café where they had their latest meeting, he tried to devise a way to make his scheme even more enticing. Mathilde, who was serving both sides, but who seemed, for the moment anyway, to be favouring the Allies, was his willing accomplice, and as they talked, it occurred to Lucas that the *Abwehr* would consider it an exemplary coup if a German spy could actually be planted inside British intelligence. If Bleicher could actually penetrate S.O.E., and have his own pipeline into the very headquarters of the enemy's espionage organization, he would have accomplished what had not been done before.

Lucas told Mathilde his idea. She was enthusiastic; but who would be this master-spy? Lucas said, "You", then he explained. The Germans, believing they could bring this off, might very well assent, and Bleicher, who did not suspect that Mathilde had betrayed him to Lucas, and who was finally convinced that she was totally loyal to him, might very well see this as his golden opportunity: on top of being able to capture a British General, plus a coterie of important underground leaders, he would also have his own secret agent inside S.O.E.

On the other hand, according to Lucas, Mathilde would escape from France, would be safely beyond the reach of the Germans. Once she reached London, she could tell all she knew to British Intelligence, which should go a long way towards effecting her reinstatement in the good graces of the Allies.

It was more than simply a bizarre scheme; it was also somewhat beyond credibility, except for one thing; the amoral ambition of the Germans, and Mathilde Carré. She could now visualize herself as the greatest master spy of the war, perhaps even of the century, while Bleicher and his *Abwehr* associates could rejoice over the prospect of someday revealing that they had been able to plant their own secret agent in the very heart of British Intelligence.

There was one more consideration. A sanguine motivation

for Lucas, which he did not mention to Mathilde, although, later, he made no secret of it to Ben Cowburn and Roger Cottin. Once he got her into an Allied boat or aircraft bound for London, Bleicher's '*Kleines Kätchen*' would never again be able to betray another patriot to his death, and instead of the Germans penetrating S.O.E., Lucas would have destroyed their 'turned-around' radio facilities, would have discredited Hugo Bleicher, 'the ace of the *Abwehr*', and would have turned over to Allied Intelligence the double agent who had done more than any other French person to hamper the development of the French resistance.

15

The Best Laid Plans

For Mathilde, who had Bleicher won over so well that he was now assuming the full initiative, as though the scheme to send Lucas to London to fetch back a British General were entirely his own idea, the duel of wits was more than half won.

When she left Lucas with the new proposal, the one by which she would accompany him to London, she was astute enough to encourage Bleicher into discussing what must now be done in order to get Lucas safely out of France, and at the height of his enthusiasm, to insinuate this even more daring suggestion: if she accompanied Luacs, and through him could become established in the British Intelligence organization, in F-Section of S.O.E., for example, Bleicher would then have his own spy at the very source of the enemy's Intelligence network.

Bleicher thought the idea was superb. He told Mathilde he would take this fresh idea up with his superiors, and meanwhile she was to meet Lucas again, and work with him in devising the means by which the British would arrange to have him taken off the Continent.

She hurried to her next rendezvous, and told Lucas that Bleicher had thought that latest 'escape' development was a capital idea. She and Lucas then worked out the message to be sent to London requesting that he be picked up. There was to be no mention of taking Mathilde out, too.

It was Lucas's idea that in order to avoid the delay this suggestion might entail, London need not be told in advance that Lucas was not returning alone. It could have created an awkward situation if London had decided to send over one of its light aircraft, but Lucas's idea was that the pick-up should be accomplished by sea, in which case a little added weight would make no difference.

Hugo Bleicher, meanwhile, had put the latest proposal to his superiors. After some consideration, all but one officer agreed to the plan. The solitary dissenter did not trust Mathilde, but he was easily argued down. After all, Mathilde had performed splendidly for the Germans. She had even risked her life by being present when some of the men she had betrayed had been apprehended. Sergeant Bleicher had been working with her since the previous year; he vouched for her without reservation.

Again, though, the Gestapo had to be consulted. And now there was a further consideration: The plan which had started out boldly, had progressed even more boldly. No German intelligence apparatus had ever managed to place agents inside the British government's espionage organizations, although the effort had been made. As a matter of fact, excepting a handful of 'deep-cover' agents, those who had been residents of Britain for many years, nearly all naturalized citizens, Germany had few secret agents in Britain at all. (In contrast, every German Intelligence organization had been penetrated by the Soviets.)

When the information reached Berlin that the *Abwehr* had a plan by which one of its V-men (or women, in this case) had an opportunity to penetrate Britain's S.O.E., Berlin decided to send a high officer to Paris to investigate. Lucas's wish to be taken off the Continent had quickly backfired, for even though the Paris headquarters of the *Abwehr* was prepared to move, word was now received to await the arrival of the officer from Berlin.

Also, the Gestapo's latest reaction was more vehement than before. Not only did the Gestapo refuse to condone the scheme, its officers were of the opinion that everyone connected with the enterprise, excluding Sergeant Bleicher, Major Eschig, and the other Germans, but not excluding Mathilde, should be taken aside and shot. This also included Roger Cottin and the burly Lancashireman, Ben Cowburn.

It may not have seemed so to Lucas, but the order to hold everything in abeyance pending the arrival of the officer from Berlin was a blessing in disguise. The Gestapo had officers in Paris who ranked Colonel Reile. If the officer from Berlin was a general, as was thought to be the case, the Gestapo could not force any edicts on the *Abwehr*.

Mathilde met Lucas to explain that Bleicher had been very pleased at the latest scheme – to get her to London with Lucas as her sponsor – but that the Gestapo was opposed to the entire idea, and finally, that nothing could not be done until the officer from Berlin arrived.

Those were harrowing days for the S.O.E. agents. They spent them creating their underground network, something they managed to do with signal success. By the time the over-shadowing matter had been resolved among the wrangling Germans, Roger Cottin and Ben Cowburn had, with some help from the otherwise occupied Lucas, worked up a very creditable espionage-sabotage organization among whose members was the same Marquis de Moustier who had earlier co-operated in *Résistance* work.

There were embryonic cells in process of formation in distant areas, as well as near, and in Paris, and the difficulty of contacting London, which had originally got Pierre de Vomécourt (Lucas) involved with Mathilde and the Germans, had been resolved by air-dropped radio equipment. This new network eventually became extensive, and it managed to survive the war almost entirely intact, without ever being penetrated. But its contribution to the adventures of Mathilde Carré were negligible, and for that reason it was soon lost sight of when Bleicher summoned Mathilde one evening, to inform her that the officer from Berlin, after acting in the capacity of advocate, and listening to all the arguments, had decided that the *Abwehr* was justified, and that Lucas's scheme – as Hugo Bleicher's idea – should be carried forward.

Mathilde was to go at once and tell Monsieur Lucas that he had been cleared to leave France. She dutifully carried this information to Lucas, along with the exuberant comment that she and Lucas had hoodwinked not only the entire *Abwehr*, but also the dreaded Gestapo, plus a very high-ranking Intelligence officer from Berlin. For Lucas, right up until the last moment, it was a matter of who was hoodwinking whom. He, the British secret agent, Bleicher, the German *Abwehr* agent, or Mathilde Carré the double, now triple, secret agent.

Ben Cowburn was present at the rendezvous when Mathilde arrived with the news, and in accordance with Lucas's earlier decision to leave France by sea, Cowburn was sent to seek a suitable place along the Brittany coast for the embarkation. He was especially suited for this assignment as a result of his earlier residence in France.

Finally, Lucas and Mathilde collaborated on the message to be sent to London, asking for an M.T.B. pick-up. It was to be said that immediate action was imperative, because the Gestapo was getting close, and this was no exaggeration, for although the Gestapo was to remain in the background of what the Germans considered an *Abwehr* affair, it knew who Lucas was, who Ben Cowburn was, and it had not changed its opinion that the best way to treat enemy secret agents was with a bullet in the back of the neck.

For Mathilde, the most bizarre adventure of her life was shortly to begin. It was not to go smoothly at all, but it would culminate in one of the most unique espionage situations of the war. She inaugurated it when she returned to Hugo Bleicher on rue de la Faisanderie to show him Lucas's message, and to explain to him that Ben Cowburn would reconnoitre the Brittany coast where the pick-up was to take place. Lucas had to wait, but at least he had the new network to keep him occupied while he awaited London's confirmation that a Motor Torpedo Boat pick-up could be arranged.

Mathilde, too, had to go through similar agonies of doubt and fear, but unlike Lucas, she at least was not at the mercy of someone who had already betrayed most of their friends, and all of their former underground allies.

For Hugo Bleicher the wait was not as peril-laden. Because he expected no treachery, his real concern was divided between worrying about London replying favourably, and German coastal defence elements rushing zealously forward at the sight of an enemy Motor Torpedo Boat, and spoiling everything.

While he could do little about the former, it was possible for his service-unit, the *Abwehr*, to contact the appropriate naval and other coastal defence commands, and brief them to the extent that, upon the night an Allied MTB appeared, it was under no circumstances to be challenged, or even actually 'seen'.

At the German end, preparations progressed satisfactorily. They may have accomplished this through a quite unexpected intrusion. It was claimed later that General von Stülpnagel, German Commander-in-Chief in Occupied France, had himself passed orders to the German Naval Commander at Brest to make certain no beach patrols or any other defence units interfered with the *Abwehr's* forthcoming covert operation.

This may have been true in a way no one in either Paris or London suspected at the time. General Karl Heinrich von Stülpnagel, who replaced his kinsman, Otto von Stülpnagel, as Commander-in-Chief in France, and the German Commander-in-Chief in Belgium, General von Falkenhausen, were together not only fiercely hostile to Adolf Hitler, but active in the secret machinations which were gathering momentum among Germany's elite high officer corps, and such civilian organizations within Germany as the trade unions, to oust Hitler, if possible, by a concerted revolt, or, if that appeared unlikely to succeed, then to assassinate him.

The secret scheme in which von Stülpnagel was heavily committed was not the only plot to eliminate *Reichsführer* Hitler, but it was the only one which could have had a bearing upon the affairs of Mathilde Carré by the spring of 1942. It was von Stülpnagel's belief, even before early 1942, that Hitler's war would result in the destruction of Germany, and by 1942, when the United States entered the conflict as an ally of Britain, von Stülpnagel's conviction was confirmed when Britain's air attacks over Germany became so devastating that entire cities within the *Reich*, and their populations, were completely laid waste.

If the *Abwehr* could successfully plant a German secret agent in a high office – Intelligence – in London, von Stülpnagel's chance of effecting contact with the enemy's Supreme Command would be greatly facilitated, but it had to be accomplished covertly, as long as Hitler lived.

It did not happen, which may have been a great tragedy, although no one can truly say what the outcome of such an affair might have been, except to note that the war dragged on another three years, at a staggering cost in lives and property. The main reason it did not succeed was because Mathilde Carré was, by the spring of 1942, no longer a German agent. But it was also possible that by early 1942 von Stülpnagel was more committed to Operation Valkyrie, the assassination of Adolf Hitler, than to seeking an accommodation with the Reich's enemies.

In any event, there were certainly strong indications that the *Abwehr's* plan to get Mathilde to London, had high-level approval. The *Abwehr's* subsequent involvement in the plots against Hitler – which eventually destroyed the organization and got its chief, Admiral Canaris, executed by being hanged naked, from a meat hook – all of which failed, as did the scheme to plant a German double agent in London, tended toward a belief that the *Abwehr* actually was, at its top-level, at any rate, concerned with ending the war.

Sergeant Hugo Bleicher would not have been privy to any high-level, secret *Abwehr* schemes, but he had his own plots, and regardless of what someone as exalted as General von Stülpnagel did, as long as Bleicher's low-level schemes prospered, he was happy. Therefore, when word eventually arrived from London that an MTB would come over to take Lucas off the Continent, Bleicher and his co-conspirators in Colonel Reile's Paris headquarters, as well as at *Abwehr* St Germain, were elated.

Bleicher told Mathilde that the Germans were wholeheartedly in support of the plan, and no trouble would come from their side. She went at once to inform Lucas. He was sanguinely pleased, his feelings no doubt paralleling those of a man told to put his hand into a nest of vipers upon the assurance that, probably, none would strike.

Generally, the most successful subterfuges were the least complicated ones. The plan to get Mathilde to London, with Lucas, was anything but uncomplicated. Mathilde, the crux of it, was a former Allied secret agent, now thought by the Germans to be their double agent, while actually she was now attempting to serve the Allies again, and betray her German employers. Lucas, the Frenchman serving British Intelligence, known for what he was to the Germans, and who knew they knew, but pretending *not* to know they knew, while loyal to the Allies, but pretending to be used by German Intelligence, had to also keep from Bleicher this knowledge, while simultaneously keeping from Mathilde the knowledge that, upon arrival in London, he meant to denounce her as a traitor.

Beyond this bewildering array of deception lurked the Gestapo, hoping something would go wrong, and beyond the Gestapo were Roger Cottin, Ben Cowburn and the members of the new *réseau*, unsure from day to day what must inevitably come out of all this.

When London wirelessed Neuilly that an MTB would arrive off the Breton coast, at a place known as Moulin de la Rive, on 12th February, at least the members of Lucas's immediate secret organization could presume they were safe; the Germans, even the relentless Gestapo, would not dare do anything at this juncture which would imperil the success of the *Abwehr's* proposed great triumph.

Then that certain inevitability which could not avoid happening in the face of all the complications, occurred, and what should have been a grimly diabolical drama, turned into something that would have been hilarious under different circumstances.

Now that all the obstacles to departure appeared to have been miraculously overcome, Hugo Bleicher briefed Mathilde on how she should act in London. She must constantly be on her guard; she must memorize certain keys so that wireless transmission to Neuilly – to Bleicher – would be identifiable as having emanated from her; she must try hard to get the names of Allied secret agents functioning on the Continent, but especially in France, and she must, above all else, convince the British that her loyalty to them had never wavered.

As for the evidence she should give them respecting general conditions in France, and also the information she should offer about the Germans, Bleicher had a series of glib statements. Finally, if Mathilde could bring back some decent English tobacco...

For her part, Mathilde had devised a plan she thought would certainly help her back into Allied good graces. If there were trouble, she told Bleicher, she really should know where a friendly German spy or two might be contacted in Britain; someone whose loyalty to the *Reich* was unquestionable, in the event she needed a 'safe-house'.

Bleicher gave her no names, which was fortunate for Germany's spies in Britain, because without any doubt Mathilde wanted those names so that she could hand them over to British Intelligence. He did, however, feed Mathilde's vanity by assuring her that when she returned in triumph after penetrating S.O.E., not only would she be honoured as perhaps the greatest secret agent of the war, but also that the Germans would show their admiration in a substantial way, by presenting her with a great amount of money.

When she accused Bleicher of not giving her the list of German spies in Britain because he did not trust her, Bleicher blandly replied that of course he trusted her, completely, but she should realize that the British were going to watch her day and night, were going to interrogate her closely, and in any case, it was not pertinent that she know, or seek to contact, any German agents.

Finally, with Ben Cowburn in place on the rugged coast of Finisterre, and the cold, bitter, short days of February moving towards the moment of embarkation, Mathilde and Lucas made their immediate plans, and she packed her black coat and red hat for the trip. Lucas was less concerned with packing than with a fresh development. It was very possible that the moment Mathilde and Lucas boarded the MTB's ship-to-shore dinghy, the Germans, who were certain to be watching the embarkation from hiding, would seize Cowburn, and if they were of the Gestapo, shoot him on the spot.

Against this possibility, Lucas decided now, to take Cowburn aboard the MTB with them, at the last moment.

Bleicher now saw to it that a pair of *Abwehr* officers were to be dispatched ahead to the coast, in full uniform, to make certain that no patrols or coast guardsmen should blunder along and upset everything. As it turned out, these two men were unable to go ahead, and finally, on Thursday evening, when Mathilde and Lucas boarded the Paris-Brest train, the two officers took the same train, but sat in a different compartment. The officers were not to stay aboard all the way to Brest, but were to leave the train at the inlet of Morlaix, secure a car there, and finish their trip in this fashion. Otherwise the Germans were to use their coast-defence vessels to prevent any ships from intruding into the path of the MTB. From the German side, all precautions were thoroughly and efficiently handled. Mathilde told Lucas with great satisfaction, that the Germans had done everything possible to ensure a safe and orderly leave-taking. Unfortunately, she could make no such prediction about the British, whose historic ineptitude at nefariousness had been the source of exasperation to Britain's enemies since the days of Benedict Arnold and earlier.

February was a bleak time of year in Paris, and upon the Brittany coast where the sea-winds made the weather even worse, it was certain to be less hospitable. Even so, the use of a MTB was more likely to result in success than the use of the customary little Lysander aircraft, this time of year.

On the long train ride from Paris to the Breton coast, through a cold, dark night, Mathilde and Lucas had ample time to talk, to plan, and to worry; at any moment the Germans could telegraph ahead and have the train stopped. But everything proceeded perfectly, right up to the point where Mathilde and Luacs left the Paris-Brest express at Guincamp, took a local train to Plouart, where they finally had to start walking.

It was quite a walk. From Plouart to the point of rendezvous at Moulin de la Rive was a distance of twenty-five miles. Cowburn met them at Plouart. He and Mathilde had suitcases. Lucas had a shoulder-pack, a rucksack, mostly filled with German editions of French newspapers, train timetables, and the like, which was not very heavy.

The unpredictable weather favoured them. After daylight, while they hiked overland, the sun came out, there was very little sea-wind, and all omens pointed to success. The fact that probably the least likely companions of the war were crossing the countryside, could almost be lost sight of: a German secret agent, a French secret agent, and a British secret agent, walking together in complete amiability.

They had a noon-day meal at a village along the way, and later, at another village, Locquirec, close to their point of rendezvous, they rested, and watched the unpredictable February weather begin to change. The wind came off the sea, wet and cold, clouds began to build up, and the sun disappeared. They went down to the point of rendezvous, saw how the sea was ominously surging – and encountered a German coast patrol. The Germans made an almost painfully obvious effort to look in every direction but the one which the three bundled-up civilians were using, and hastened away.

It began to rain. The sea pitched and darkened. The wind became violent. As the time for the MTB to appear approached, it began to look as though no light vessel would dare come close to the rugged coast.

Mathilde, drenched to the skin, clutching her suitcase, sought protection from the elements among the rocks, with Lucas and Cowburn. At the appointed moment Lucas went to the edge of the surf to signal with a small hand-torch. He received no answer, but two men in civilian clothes came walking up the beach. Lucas and Ben Cowburn went at once to meet the strangers. One of them, Lieutenant G.W. Abbott, was an S.O.E. radioman who, with his companion, Lieutenant Redding, had just been put ashore, with a transmitter, a short distance down the beach. Abbott and Redding were totally unaware of the situation they had blundered into, and when Lucas explained that the Germans were watching from somewhere close by the rocks, it was hastily decided to rush back where the Royal Navy had landed Abbott and Redding, and embark at once.

Accordingly, the four men and Mathilde ran down the beach in pouring rain, found the pair of rowboats, and in the face of the astonished Royal Navy seaman, hurled themselves aboard, while excitedly telling the seaman to row hard.

They got a few yards from the beach, out into the breakers, and both over-loaded dinghys capsized. Mathilde lost her suitcase, and was very nearly pulled out to sea, but fought desperately to reach shore, and with the others, finally managed to stand up out of the water, bedraggled, breathless, chilled to the bone.

The larger vessel signalled shoreward that it would attempt a close approach, but the sea was too high, and too dangerously full of shore-ward currents. The next signal to shore informed the stranded people that the vessel could not linger, and as it departed, the Australian officer who had been in charge of the earlier landing operations, was conspicuous even in the rain, in his Royal Navy uniform.

16
A Sequence Of Errors

The conclusion of this botched affair occurred the following day when the Australian naval officer, walking briskly across country in his Royal Naval uniform was seen by astounded French country people and the Germans, who went out and arrested him.

The pair of S.O.E. secret agents, Redding and Abbott, who made their way to the farm of a Frenchman named Geoffroy, were taken in Geoffroy's barn the following morning by Germans who had known, since the previous night, how disaster had befallen Mathilde's special *Abwehr* enterprise, and this pair of inadvertent intruders.

As for Mathilde and Lucas, they and Ben Cowburn walked dismally back to Locquirec, where they arrived before daylight, roused the local innkeeper, and after he had laid a roaring fire for them to dry out by, they assessed the magnitude of their failure, and discussed the deadly possibility that, now, the Gestapo might prevail over the *Abwehr*, and also, that the *Abwehr* might arrive at a conclusion that the scheme was no longer feasible, even without the Gestapo's help.

Without a doubt, Lucas and Cowburn were in the greatest peril. Even Mathilde, who had been so cheerful the day before, so confident, might very well decide, privately, not to pursue this affair further; might very well revert to her former role as the *Abwehr's* advocate, dangerous as that would now be, for her as well as for the two men.

She had certainly suffered as much, and even more, than had the men. She was still the pivotal figure; whatever she decided to do would determine the fate of the men with her that grey, dismal dawn at Locquirec. Also, in the course of her battle with the sea, she had received several bad cuts about the feet and legs, from sharp stones. These bled a fair amount, and although both Lucas and Cowburn were helpful and solicitous, that was no guarantee that she would repay kindness in kind. She had repaid it at other times in a completely reverse manner.

At least the Germans did not arrive. Obviously, although they knew everything that had happened, and had busily rounded-up the other participants, their discretion in not driving to the inn at Locquirec was in accordance with *Abwehr* instructions.´

Their host at the inn, while entirely willing to let them dry out, and just as willing to prepare them a very welcome hot breakfast, was not willing to have them linger at his establishment one moment longer than was absolutely necessary; a man did not have to possess the sophistication of a Parisian to be instinctively aware that those three people, only one of whom was obviously French, who had gone down to the beach the previous night, carrying suitcases, in a raging storm, and who had subsequently returned, drenched, battered, and dispirited, were not ordinary travellers. The Germans could be very severe, even to uninvolved innkeepers, and one never knew when they would arrive out front, helmeted, armed, and determined to be unpleasant. The innkeeper then asked his guests to leave.

They left, but instead of heading back for Plouart, it was decided to make one more effort, and they accordingly walked to the next village, Lanmeur, in the still inclement weather. By the time they got to Lanmeur, they were drenched again. To make matters worse, Mathilde could barely hobble along. The men supported her much of the way but she would not consent to be carried. Also, without seeing anyone, they knew they were being followed. Altogether, it was a very miserable affair.

At Lanmeur, Cowburn and Lucas sought a small inn where they might again dry out, and get something to eat, while Mathilde went to a nearby German coast-defence facility and telephoned Bleicher in Paris to explain what had happened. He was solicitous. He also agreed that the forlorn trio of bedraggled spies should lie over one more night, in the off chance that the S.O.E. might send over another MTB.

They rested at Lanmeur throughout the day. Mathilde's cuts were properly looked after, they slept, ate, and by nightfall were ready to return to Locquirec for another long wait in the lee of the rocky escarpments.

This second night was bitterly cold. They huddled together until about four o'clock in the morning, repeatedly, at spaced intervals, giving the pre-arranged signal by hand-torch.

Nothing happened. There were no answering signals from offshore. Finally, with dawn close, they clambered back dispiritedly over the rocks and returned to Locquirec, stiff with cold and sunk in the gloom of bitter disappointment.

For Mathilde there was physical pain as well as disappointment, and it may have been typical of her nature that, as her companions on that night were to recall later, she never once complained. She, who had caused others anguish, suffered considerably during this interlude when she was desperately seeking to escape from France, and she accepted both the pain and the bitter disappoinment without a single complaint.

Finally, convinced there was to be no rescue, Mathilde told Lucas they must return to Paris. She thought they might be able to inaugurate a fresh plan – providing the Germans were not now tired of the entire farce. Of course, the German surveillance team, which Mathilde did not see, was also preparing to return and report.

However, there was one risk Lucas was unprepared to take. Ben Cowburn, who was not actually important to Hugo Bleicher's plan, and who was known to be under a Gestapo death sentence, could only be walking into disaster by returning to Paris. If he fled, he might be able to reach safety. If he remained with Lucas he had no chance at all. Lucas told him to make a run for it.

Actually, Cowburn's chances of reaching England were good. He had friends in France. He was also known to Lucas's influential and rather extensive family. And finally, in those times, very few French people minded anyone's business but their own; a stalwart Lancashireman who in no way resembled the French, could pass along with an excellent probability of being studiously ignored by everyone but informers and Germans.

. He made it, eventually, with discreet aid along the way – once from an American in Vichy – and although he had to traverse over half the length of France to reach the Spanish frontier, in a land swarming with Germans, and the German-controlled French police – called Milice – Cowburn finally reached Spain.

Lucas's last word to Cowburn had been to wireless a warning about Mathilde the moment he reached Spain, which Cowburn did, then, by way of Madrid and Lisbon, Cowburn finally reached England. (Subsequently, this courageous secret agent was parachuted into France again, in early June, 1942, with another agent, Ernest Wilkinson, code-named Alexandre – and narrowly escaped with his life when Wilkinson was arrested. Cowburn was still active in the French underground when the war ended, and although the Germans sought hard to apprehend him, he was never captured, and survived the war.)

Finally then, Lucas and Mathilde returned to Paris from Brittany, arriving back in the capital of Occupied France, on 15th February, Lucas to go in search of Roger Cottin, and a place to stay, Mathilde to the 'Castel' residence at 26 rue de La Faisanderie, where she was welcomed back by a sympathetic Hugo Bleicher.

She told Bleicher what she thought of the British who sent the wrong boat to the wrong stretch of the French coast, then neglected to ever send the right one. She also said that Cowburn had left the party after all their dismal and exasperating misadventures, and she did not blame him. She further told Bleicher that after being nearly drowned, badly cut on the rocks at Moulin de la Rive, and in peril of catching pneumonia two nights in a row, she was heartily disgusted with the whole affair. If it was bait, Bleicher took it. He assured her that they would yet succeed; that she must rest and recover, and they would try again.

Lucas, meanwhile, using another *réseau* transmitter, sent off an indignant message to London, but although the British were undoubtedly superb procrastinators, it was difficult to see how they could be at fault for France's bad weather.

In London, Lucas's disappointment was no less than the disappointment of F-section, S.O.E., which had looked forward to Lucas's arrival with high anticipation, and accordingly, another pick-up was scheduled. Lucas was notified of this on 18th February, with the MTB rescue to be effected one night later, at about midnight of the 19th, or shortly after midnight, which would be on 20th February.

That certainly did not allow much time, but since London transmitted this information through the German-controlled 'Victoire' receiver at Neuilly, it ensured German co-operation, which of course, would minimize the obstacles. Bleicher was enthusiastic. Especially since he had been taken into London's confidence to the extent that he was informed, through Neuilly, that a different area of contact was to be used. The MTB would arrive off Pointe de Behit, below the town of Trebeurden, also along the Breton coast, but some distance from the scene of the earlier disaster.

He cajoled Mathilde, whose injuries, while not serious, were still painful. He offered her all the same assurances again; money, fame, admiration, and of course his personal gratitude. She met with Lucas, worked out their altered itinerary and once again they entrained for Finisterre, from Paris, and once again the *Abwehr* accompanied them, in a separate compartment of the same train.

They left the train at Lannion, in Côtes-Du-Nord, for a bus ride to the town of Trebeurden. How their German shadows accomplished this leg of the trip was left to them. From Trebeurden they would have another long walk, this time of less than half the distance to that other point of rendezvous, a mere ten miles. At least it did not rain.

Upon arriving at Trebeurden, at the end of the day, they went to a local inn for a pleasant dinner, their last in France for some time they hoped, and after nightfall they set out on foot through the darkness – with no guide and no familiarity with the countryside – and of course got lost.

Eventually, they came upon a village named Servel. It was almost midnight when they arrived there and secured directions from a native. Fortunately, Servel was in the correct general direction. They hurried forth through a rather untamed, primitive coastal area, and ultimately reached their destination, breathless and fearful that, this time it would be their fault, not the Royal Navy's fault, if a contact was not made.

It was one o'clock in the morning when Lucas walked to the edge of the surf to signal with his hand-torch. He did this several times, and from out across the dark-rolling sea, there was no answer. He returned to where Mathilde waited, huddled against the cold. They stood together in abject dismay.

Lucas went forth and signalled again, and again, until about four-thirty in the morning. There was no answer, the sea was empty of boats of any kind, local fishermen, German patrol vessels, or British MTBs. Demoralized, they set out to return to Lannion. They had a meal at Trebeurden, then boarded the bus for Lannion. There was not much to say. Mathilde was agreeable to waiting until the next night for a final effort.

It was a long day, in Lannion. All the fears and doubts returned. Somewhere nearby, would be at least one *Abwehr* man keeping them under surveillance. At any time Bleicher might contact him to end the farce. On the other side, after so many false starts, there was reason to suspect that the British might also have decided not to keep the appointment. Worst of all was the excellent possibility that the British would not arrive at midnight of 20th/21st, which was a day later than the scheduled rendezvous.

At this juncture Lucas, who was completely at the mercy of his enemies and Mathilde, could not have imagined a worse situation to be in, and as the bleak winter day drew to its early close, and as he and a subdued Cat went to dinner in Lannion, Lucas was entitled to believe that there was a very good chance that the MTB would not arrive, and that, finally, the Gestapo would triumph, in which case he would probably be dead by dawn.

They boarded the bus for the coast, after dinner, rode stoically to whatever was in store for them, and after the long walk to Pointe de Bihit, again in bitter cold, kept their exasperating vigil.

Without being rescued. Without even raising a light out to sea in response to Lucas's desperately hopeful, and continuous signals.

They waited as they had done before, until shortly before dawn, to abandon the rendezvous and hike back to Trebeurden, stiff with cold, and thoroughly demoralized.

They did not try again. If the British had not come on the second night, when they had reason to believe they would not have been expected, there was even less reason to believe they would come on the third night.

Dispiritedly they rode the old bus back to Lannion, and from there entrained for Paris. It was more plausible than ever to expect the Germans to yield in disgust, now, and cancel the entire enterprise.

When Mathilde walked into the flat at rue de la Faisanderie she was astonished by Hugo Bleicher's greeting. The *Abwehr* officer, Captain Heinz A. Eckert, who had shadowed Mathilde and Lucas so painstakingly, had already returned to report. The British motor torpedo boat had arrived, and exactly on schedule. It had signalled the shore, and the *Abwehr* man's disgust was almost strong enough to motivate him to climb down to the little hidden cove where the two stupid spies were waiting, and tell them to move on around a little sheltering headland where they could then see the signals from the sea, and the MTB's crewmen would be able to see Lucas's signals from the shore. It had been that close.

Mathilde duly reported to Lucas what had happened, while Bleicher and the *Abwehr* officer who had been risking pneumonia throughout all the abortive rescues, burly Captain Heinz Eckert, held a conference. It was decided that when the next attempt was made German thoroughness would be substituted for French inefficiency. But elsewhere the repeated failures, and the loss of a naval officer, four seamen, plus two S.O.E. agents, Redding and Abbott, and all the cargo the agents had brought ashore with them including the radio transmitters as well as an assortment of weapons, and 600,000 francs, had F-section in a quandary. It seemed in London, that there was treachery involved.

Hugo Bleicher saved the day. He wirelessed London over the 'Victoire' radio at Neuilly that Abbott and Redding were safe, that all the money and supplies were now in the hands of S.O.E. secret agents, and that the naval personnel would be smuggled out of France at the earliest opportunity. London was placated. Bleicher sent forth a request for another pickup. Acknowledgement was to be through the BBC, when the MTB left England.

This time the rendezvous was to take place on the night of 26th February, or, if it occurred after midnight, on the 27th. The rendezvous was to be the Pointe de Bihit, as before, near a large escarpment known as the Rock Mignon.

This time Bleicher, himself, went with Captain Eckert to make sure there were no more failures. This time the British, also, were intent upon success. Colonel Maurice Buckmaster, head of F-section, sent along Major Nicholas Boddington to supervise the entire function.

Mathilde and Lucas returned to the rendezvous by the same route they had used before. They rode a train from Paris to Lannion, a bus from Lannion to Trebeurden, and after nightfall, they walked the ten miles to the cove where they were to meet the MTB.

Hugo Bleicher and Heinz Eckert made the same trip, but discreetly, and were in position before midnight, hidden in the rocks, bundled in their great-coats, when Lucas stepped forth to give the signal from shore.

This time there was an answering signal from out in the darkness across the water.

17
London, 1942

The successful contact was made when Major Boddington came ashore with eight armed seamen. Offshore, the British light vessel, commanded by Lieutenant Dunstan Curtis, lay to, ready at a moment's notice to lend assistance. None was needed. Major Boddington, revolver in hand, met Mathilde and Lucas on the beach, deployed the armed seamen around him, and under the eyes of Sergeant Bleicher and Captain Eckert, in the overhead rocks, escorted the spies to his boat, got them aboard, and this time returned to the offshore vessel without incident, through a co-operative sea.

After so many false starts, the pick-up had finally been accomplished. On board the MTB, where there was no provision for females, and where it had not been known one was coming aboard, an astonished and dismayed seaman looked at Mathilde and said, "Oh, Christ, it's a bloody woman!" Thus was Mathilde welcomed to her new role as a triple agent in the service of the Allies.

Lieutenant Curtis set his course for home, and the great-coated Germans in the rocks could finally stand erect to watch the departure. Mathilde did not share everyone else's relief because she was not much of a sailor. As the small vessel rode the choppy sea, she went to a bunk below and remained there with a queasy stomach throughout the four-hour voyage, reappearing on deck only when the MTB reached a berth in Dartmouth Harbour.

Colonel Buckmaster was on shore, waiting to greet Lucas. He shared the earlier surprise of the Royal Navy seaman when Mathilde stepped ashore, hand-bag in hand, but the colonel was a bland, unflappable individual. He took his small party to an early breakfast, where Mathilde did less justice to the food than did the hungry men. But Mathilde's spirits rose

again, on shore. She teased Major Boddington, and impressed
Colonel Buckmaster with her confidence.

She acted as though she had achieved a great personal
triumph, which, in a sense, she had. Behind her, in France,
was the trusting Hugo Bleicher, and those in the *Abwehr*, of
higher rank who shared Bleicher's optimism. Also, in France,
were the people she had betrayed. One at least of whom was
dead, and others who would shortly die, as well as many
others who would now begin their years-long struggle to stay
alive under conditions it would be difficult to imagine.

From Dartmouth, the S.O.E. entourage headed for London
by way of Paignton, where word was telephoned ahead for
preparations to be made for the reception of Mathilde, the
unexpected *voyageur*. This reception was to include close, but
discreet, security. Lucas and Colonel Buckmaster had held a
brief council at Dartmouth; Lucas had told the colonel that
Mathilde had been a double agent for the Germans.

Nothing the colonel said or did on the way to London
aroused any misgivings in Mathilde. The British method of
handling spies was as different from the German method as
night was different from day. In fact, when Matilde finally
arrived in London, her first view of the great, war-mauled
metropolis which stood as the heart and the symbol of
everything the Germans opposed, she found that a woman
from F-section had been detailed to act as her chaperon. This
woman was also to act as her guard. And British
consideration had gone farther. There was new clothing;
under-garments, night attire, even face powder and a tooth
brush. She was received as a valued and cherished ally, and to
someone with Mathilde's preening variety of vanity, it was
exactly what she had expected. She was, after all, by her own,
and Hugo Bleicher's assessment, the greatest spy of the war.

To the British she was not the Cat, and certainly not *Kleines
Kätzchen*, she was, and remained, Mme Mathilde Carré.

A unique factor, up to this point, was that none of those
various warnings about Mathilde had reached London, before
she and Lucas arrived there. They had been sent from such
divergent places as Vichy and Madrid, Berne and Lisbon. The
senders included Phillipe de Vomècourt, Lucas's brother, an

American Naval attaché, the French underground, and of course Lucas himself. It did not really matter once Mathilde was in S.O.E. custody, but it created misgivings about the reliability of the French-British espionage contact.

On the other hand, as soon as it was possible to do so, a message was sent from London to the German-controlled radio facility at Neuilly, and was received without delay, announcing that Lucas and 'Victoire' had reached London safely.

The three sections of Allied Intelligence which were concerned with 'Victoire', S.O.E – F-Section the War Office Intelligence Service, and the Polish Intelligence Service, were duly informed of Mathilde's association with German Military Intelligence – the *Abwehr*. Presumably this information was also made available to the S.O.E.'s parent organization, the Ministry of Economic Warfare, and to the French Committee of Liberation's *Bureau Central de Renseignements et d'Action*, General de Gaulle's free French Intelligence Service, whose prickly sensitivity made cooperation between the B.C.R.A., and the S.O.E. – in fact with all Allied Intelligence organizations – a sporadic affair.

Of course, Mathilde was unaware of any of this, and she probably did not even suspect that she was not really considered a valued Ally agent, during her first few conferences with British officers. She would have had little reason to believe she was considered suspect. When the Germans had initially apprehended her, they had sent her to a bleak cell at La Santé, when the British had her in custody, she was given, besides a new wardrobe and other creature-comforts, which were of such inestimable value to Mathilde, a delightful, roomy apartment overlooking Hyde Park on Bayswater Road, which had two airy bedrooms – one for her chaperon – a modern bathroom, a lounge and kitchen, and an excellent third-floor view of bomb-devastated London.

She was taken to dinner by her hosts, treated to a war-time luxury, fine French wine, and was shown courtesy and consideration. She was encouraged to talk, which she did, about her French-German connections. She was flattered and admired by those suave English executives of British

Intelligence, whose steel-trap minds were sifting everything she told them, extracting the raw, basic truths, and Hugo Bleicher's earlier blandness had to appear adolescent by comparison.

Her chaperon also encouraged Mathilde to talk, in the privacy of their pleasant apartment – which was festooned with microphones. Mathilde, who had never been reticent, was in her glory. She had a German secret code, which she willingly gave to the British. They used it to send messages back to Neuilly in 'Victoire's' name. They also used it successfully for a time, to feed false information to the *Abwehr*.

As though determined to blot out completely the memory of her betrayals, Mathilde now cooperated with British Intelligence as wholeheartedly as she had formerly cooperated with the Germans. She made lists of German intelligence agents, particularly those of the *Abwehr* in Paris, and at St Germain-en-Laye. She withheld nothing, although she was never open about her betrayals. And Mathilde *did* know quite a bit about the Germans in France. She had picked up considerable information of a worthwhile nature while at *Abwehr* St Germain, as well as at the Cattery; the Germans, and especially Hugo Bleicher, had, over the months, come to trust her enough to speak quite openly in her presence.

During this period, the association between Mathilde and Pierre de Vomécourt – Lucas – gradually faded. Lucas, who also had much to tell, and whose powers of observation as well as general intelligence, far exceeded the same attributes in Mathilde, provided British Intelligence with a graphic and full explanation of over-all conditions in France. He had conferences with S.O.E.'s Director of Operations, General Colin McVean Gubbins, as well as his own immediate superior, Colonel Buckmaster. He also met Lord Selborne, the new Minister of Economic Warfare, as well as General Sir Alan Brooke, chief of the Imperial General Staff, and Anthony Eden.

It was said of Lucas that, being the first agent of prominence of F-section S.O.E., to return from France, he was something of·a celebrity. But, true or not, it was his desire to return to France at the earliest possible opportunity, where his family, his brothers, and his associate, Roger Cottin, still existed in peril.

Accordingly, Pierre de Vomécourt was air-dropped into France on April Fool's day, 1942. He landed in a tree only a very short distance from the Brignac estate of his brother, Phillippe. No one told Mathilde he had returned to France, and in fact, the Germans were deliberately fed misleading and innocuous information to mask his arrival.

He and Mathilde met once more, in a courtroom, but by then both had been prisoners so long there was an unbridgeable abyss between them. After that, they never met again.

Lucas was finally captured by the Germans, through a fluke. As soon as possible after returning to France, he contacted Roger Cottin, and resumed his zealous work with the underground. When the Germans caught a courier, known to Roger Cottin, the man had on his person papers indicating that Lucas was again in France. As soon as Hugo Bleicher heard this, he gave orders for Roger to be picked up at once. He had to verify that Lucas was, indeed, back, because if it were true, and he had come secretly, then, obviously, neither Mathilde, nor the British General officer, were going to arrive, which meant, bluntly, that Bleicher had been betrayed.

Roger was apprehended, with other members of a fledgling *réseau*, and although Cottin would tell the Germans nothing, another member of the network told Bleicher where Lucas was. The customary carload of *Abwehr* men went forth, and made the capture. Subsequently, during interrogations, Lucas lost a number of teeth. He was put in a dark cell at Fresnes Prison for nine months, before being sent to Colditz Prison compound. He was confronted by Bleicher with a charge that Mathilde had betrayed the *Abwehr* – and her German lover – without ever confirming the truth of this allegation. He was liberated in April of 1945 when the United States Ninth Army crossed the Elbe River. (He died in Paris, a much-decorated hero of France, in 1965.)

For Mathilde, the loss of her companion of those harrowing, cold nights on the Brittany coast, was a small thing. She spent her days with officers of British Intelligence, and her nights, comfortably secure, at the Porchester Gate apartment. There was still no indication that she was an Allied prisoner. Quite the contrary. She, and her chaperon, went shopping. (S.O.E.'s offices on Baker Street were just around the corner from Selfridges.) As for the interrogations, Mathilde was open and candid in all areas, excepting those touching upon her personal acts of betrayal and treachery. These question-and-answer periods were usually conducted at Mathilde's apartment. She was never allowed to visit S.O.E.'s offices. Not that this aroused her suspicions in the least. She was certain the reason her British interrogators visited her at the apartment was because she was a very highly regarded secret agent – an exalted master (or mistress) of espionage, the most valued spy of the war – and that she was therefore entitled to a degree of homage and respect.

She and her chaperon also toured the city. Mathilde was an incorrigible sight-seer. She was enchanted by London's French restaurants, was awed by the squares of levelled buildings, was delighted by parks, and astonished to discover that, contrary to the German-controlled news broadcasts she had listened to in Paris, the British were not balancing upon the brink of extinction, amid the total collapse of all their cherished institutions. London, was, by the summer and autumn of 1942, beginning to clean up the debris, for while the sirens still wailed at night, the saturation *Luftwaffe* bombings Air Marshal Göring, and *Reichsführer* Hitler had been so positive would batter Britain into submission, had failed in their purpose, and the Germans were no longer willing to make a new effort.

Mathilde saw the Nelson plinth, Piccadilly, St Paul's Cathedral, which had not escaped the attention of the *Luftwaffe*, and Westminster Abbey, symbols of the faith of a great people in a great faith. She wanted her chaperon to show her the best shops. She also had to visit a dentist, and, more happily, she went to the hair-dresser.

For several weeks British Intelligence indulged her. She came to accept all the studied courtesies as her due. At one of the smart shops Mathilde was fascinated, child-like, by a black velvet choker with a red flower on it. She bought two, one for herself, one for her chaperon. She appeared for her daily rounds of interrogation well-dressed and properly groomed, always poised and confident. Even the plainclothesmen who shadowed her on every outing, and who stood guard outside the apartment, she accepted as part of the War Office's elaborate system for protecting her. That she was a prisoner did not dawn on her for quite a while.

She had, by this time, perfected the defence she would adhere to throughout all the years ahead: she had been an unfortunate creature of circumstance, neither of her own making, nor amenable to her control. She was simply a victim of war; a person, like everyone else, who had to survive as best she could.

She had no trouble convincing herself of this, but at least once, in a crowded London restaurant, it appeared that others did not believe it. She had been in England a month by the time this unpleasantness occurred, and all those belated warnings concerning her, had by then reached London, and among London's hordes of fugitives, and refugee Poles and French, it was generally known, at least by the Poles and French who had any connections with the underground networks, that Mathilde Carré was a traitor. She was recognized while at lunch with her chaperon by a Polish exile. He went to her table and in a violent outburst accused Mathilde of treachery, in a scene that astounded the other diners, and appeared about to erupt into a physical attack. Mathilde's protectors moved in quickly, and she was hastened out of the restaurant.

Gradually, inevitably, Mathilde began to chafe at the close surveillance. The only times she appeared to be free was when she asked to visit specific tourist attractions, or when she expressed a desire to see a particular café or night club. The British allowed her some latitude, hoping that her request might be based upon a wish to meet a German agent, but nothing of this nature ever occurred. If German agents in London knew of Mathilde Carré, they avoided her.

What abetted British suspicion was Mathilde's red hat. She wore it often, and usually while sightseeing. It was suspected of being a signal for German agents. Evidently it was not. At any rate, she was never contacted by enemy agents, and the British managed to expose her as often as she was willing to be exposed, without a stranger ever approaching her.

Eventually, when British Intelligence was satisfied that it had gleaned about all it could, Mathilde's movements were restricted, and she reacted to this in a typical manner. She complained that instead of being treated as a valued secret agent, the British attitude seemed to be one of distrust and disapproval, and she resented this, because she had certainly co-operated with them, had certainly proved herself a very clever and valuable Allied secret agent.

The charade continued a little longer. Mathilde was valuable even after being pumped dry of information, because as long as she thought of herself as an Allied agent, she helped transmit messages to Bleicher, by way of Neuilly, in a manner she alone could do best. Also, at this time, early summer, 1942, the war's tempo was again increasing, and someone like Mathilde Carré could help assess German, as well as French, reaction to the turning of the tide. The Americans, for example, committed to a two-ocean war, across the Pacific as well as across the Atlantic, began arriving in Britain, finally, and their Air Corps (later, air 'force') joined the R.A.F. in some very devastating air attacks against the Continent. Paris, which had suffered sporadic damage to this time, like Berlin, and the Saar Valley, was attacked by the Americans, by day, and the British by night, but the actual saturation bombings were still a year away. Even so, it was possible to stun the Germans, who had been faced by only a courageous handful of fighter aircraft over England during the Battle of Britain. The British night attack on Cologne, 30-31st May 1942, appalled the *Luftwaffe's* hierarchy. Everyone had been saying Britain's Royal Air Force had been battered to the ground, but on that night 1000 British bombers came across the Channel, and all but forty two returned, after laying waste great industrial areas of Germany.

Mathilde's reaction to an increasingly powerful Allied thrust was enthusiastic. Now, she again wanted the Allies to triumph, and without a doubt this was her genuine wish. But the British S.O.E., increasingly busy as the war ceased to be a

matter of defence, and also because it had other agents –
dependable ones – in France, and elsewhere on the Continent,
began to feel less inclined to tie up a chaperon, several sets of
guards, and stand the expense of Mathilde's apartment, once
her usefulness had passed.

There may have been some reluctance on S.O.E.'s part, to
do anything with Mathilde as long as Lucas was operating
again in France, but when the news was flashed to F-section
that he had been captured, S.O.E.'s last reason for humouring
Mathilde was gone. Even assuming that the Germans would
fail to compel Lucas to tell them that Mathilde had again
changed sides, was again serving the Allies, the fact that he
had appeared alone in France would certainly not go
unnoticed by Hugo Bleicher. Mathilde's value was gone. She
and Lucas had been scheduled to return together, with a
British officer of General rank. Instead Mathilde had not
returned at all, there was no General officer, and Lucas had
arrived surreptitiously, had at once become involved in a new
network, and was obviously no longer involved with Mathilde.
The British had no difficulty in guessing *Abwehr* reaction.
Henceforth, even the 'turned-around' wireless facility at
Neuilly would be wary of 'Victoire' broadcasts.

The entire affair had lasted six weeks, Mathilde's shortest
tour of service so far, in her capacity as single agent, double
agent, and finally, triple agent.

A team of plainclothesmen appeared at the apartment,
asked Mathilde to accompany them, and although at first she
thought she was to be taken to another rendezvous, perhaps to
be interrogated, when it dawned upon her that she was not
being humoured, but was being given a direct order, she was
enraged. The plainclothesmen were not especially impressed.
They hustled Mathilde to a car and delivered her to Holloway
Jail.

Finally, for Mathilde Carré, the delusion ended. But she
was alive, and in fact she was to continue in that estate while
many people she had directly and indirectly betrayed, and
thousands more she never knew, and therefore never had a
chance to betray, died every week; sometimes that many died
every day.

In prison, where the facilities were rather different than

they had been at the flat overlooking Hyde Park, but where they were also a vast improvement over La Santé, Mathilde denounced the S.O.E., as well as the British whom she said had betrayed her. She calumniated the Allies and said she would welcome an opportunity to kill Colonel Buckmaster.

She raged at her jailers, insulted the matrons, refused to co-operate, and repeatedly claimed that she had served the Allies well and bravely, and they in turn had repaid her with betrayal.

She wrote denunciatory letters, particularly to the people of S.O.E., including Colonel Buckmaster. She became busily occupied with a personal journal, a diary of justification, and through this medium, she was able to crystallize, in her own mind, the tactics of defence she would adhere to in the days ahead.

It probably did not enter her head that she could be put to death; the English did not do things like that. The Germans did, but not the English. But the English did do things like that. Treason, especially in time of war, is punishable under British law by execution.

It was not done as peremptorily, in Britain, as it was done on the Continent. The British had no corollary, no *nacht und nebel*, or the bullet in the back of the neck without trial, but even as Mathilde was furiously denouncing her captors, they, in turn, were discussing her fate in the light of high treason, punishable by death.

18

Towards Death Or Vindication

Mathilde's life had rarely been dull, possibly excepting the period she spent in North Africa, and even then, as a bride, the boredom had its mitigating moments. But from this point onward, for almost seven years, Mathilde was to learn what ennui really was. She was kept at Holloway Jail during the period when the War Office sought a solution to her case. It was suggested that she be brought to trial in England on a charge of treason, but there were specific, as well as awkward, draw-backs. One, of course lay rooted in the fact that her treachery had taken place in France, essentially against the French. But even more to the point was that to try her on a capital charge, in which, if found guilty, she could very well be put to death, would entail something the War Office, and particularly the British Intelligence community, did not want – secret agents as court-room witnesses at a public hearing.

The decision, finally, was to keep her in prison until the war ended, and review her case at that time. Accordingly, she was transferred from Holloway to Aylesbury Prison.

She seemed to lose interest in the war, and in this regard she belonged to a very small minority, for as 1942 wore along, the mounting Allied efforts, in Russia, in Africa, and in Europe, aroused fresh hopes in all the subjugated lands, but especially in Europe. By mid 1943, despite Germany's almost superhuman effort to halt the flow of material and troops across the Atlantic from America to Britain, the supply convoys continued to reach Britain, heavily guarded, and by the end of 1943 the essentials for an invasion of *Festung Europa* were stock-piling. The Battle of the Atlantic would not end until the last months of the war, but it ceased to be a one-sided contest by 1943.

Elsewhere, too, the same months which were so critical to the stocky, green-eyed French woman, were equally critical to the combatants. In the Soviet Union, the failures, shortcomings, and disasters of 1941, began to be remedied by 1942. By 1943, in Leningrad alone, where as many as 4000 people had died daily during the previous winter under the German siege, until the city's population had dropped from three million to somewhat less than one million, the unyielding resistance eventually wore the Germans down. At the bloody battle for Stalingrad, which began in the autumn of 1942, and resulted in a major defeat for the Germans (with casualties set at about a quarter of a million men) there appeared a light at the end of the tunnel for the Allies.

For Mathilde all the incredible din and stress was as nothing. She was comfortable at Aylesbury, with plenty of time to work on her journal. In July, 1943, Benito Mussolini's government fell and he was arrested. Mathilde was revising some aspects of her diary. The invasion of France from across the Channel appeared imminent, the Allies owned the air space above the Continent, Russian armies were battering the Germans in a relentless war of attrition. Mathilde wrote letters to her brother, and to her parents in Paris. When 1943 drew to a close, with the tide at long last turning so devastatingly against the Germans, that even *Reichsführer* Hitler's General Staff had lost hope, Mathilde's days ran on in peace and quiet. And finally, D-day arrived – 6th June 1944. From then on the war became a bitter, deadly contest of might versus might, with Hitler's splendid *Luftwaffe* scarcely able to take to the air, and with his triumphant *Wehrmacht* reduced to waging war as though it were a guerilla band. The war was lost for Hitler's Third Reich one year before Hitler's sycophant, and great admirer, Grand Admiral Karl Doenitz signed unconditional surrender terms for Germany, on 7th May 1945.

For a moment, an exhausted world was silent. Then came the moment of jubilation. The cataclysmic cost would be totalled later, but the actual total cost would not be measurable for a quarter century. As for the soldiers, sailors, and airmen, the time had finally come to remove the uniform, but for the so-called 'war criminals', the worst was yet to come. Mathilde was hardly a 'war criminal' in the sense that Germany's career butchers were, and as far as the Allies were concerned, with more spectacular court hearings such as the Nuremberg trials shortly to begin, Mathilde Carré was nothing more than a liability.

She was handed over to the French without being brought before the bar in England. Her last trip between England and France was made on a very unspectacular Channel ferry, in the company of Scotland Yard detectives.

At Boulogne, she was delivered to the French authorities as though she were a common felon. There were no highly colourful secret agents, no stalwart men in war-worn uniforms, no fiercely contending ideologies, just a small, sturdy French woman being delivered by British detectives to the police authorities of her native land.

She was taken to the prison at rue des Saussaies in Paris. She knew the place. By 1945 prisons were no novelty to Mathilde Carré. Altogether, during her extended confinement, first in England then in France, at both La Santé and Rennes, Mathilde spent close to seven years as a prisoner in five different establishments of incarceration.

Her eyesight, which had never been good, got steadily worse during those years. Her coarse black hair showed a little grey, and the pale olive skin which in her girlhood had tanned so bewitchingly in North Africa, became sallow. But her expression was unchanged. She considered herself a martyr, a heroic, misunderstood patriot who had been terribly betrayed. In all the ways that really counted, Mathilde had not changed at all.

There were people who felt sorry for her, and at least one of them, her mother, loudly and indignantly carped the same defence that Mathilde also used. It was shallow, insincere, and succeeded in deluding no one, unless it were other people with the same irrational mentality.

Mathilde spent three and a half years in French prisons awaiting her turn in the trial courts. France, more than most of the other conquered lands, had been devastated by war.

Foremost, naturally, was the matter of re-establishing the functions of government; next came the re-building, the re-ordering, the political, social, and educational re-structuring. Nearly as much time was required to re-order France, as it had taken to shatter it, and in some ways, considerably more time was required. Meanwhile, the crowded prisons with their German war criminals, their vast number of collaborators, were required to await the slow-turning of the wheels of French justice.

As before, in England, Mathilde used her time to polish the diary, to re-write specific passages, and to develop a writing style slanted towards arousing sympathy. She had, she wrote, "suffered so much" and "did not know how to find words to express this profound and infinite pain". She did "not want to suffer any longer". Of her unique sexuality, she wrote that, "there still exists in me this animal pleasure of the body which my soul disdains yet which I desire . . .".

For those she had voluntarily sent to their deaths in Germany, or to the horrors of the concentration camps, she wrote that although "you are dead or in prison or separated from me, I am faithful to you all and to our ideals".

She was a well-educated, literate person, which helped immensely when she wrote such things as, "Each of you went out of my life one day, in so many different ways . . . and my life closes down around all your dear faces and my dreams guard you on their wings".

It would have been impossible, years after the war, for people who had never known Mathilde, but who read excerpts from her journal, not to be compassionate towards her – if they never heard her speak as she spoke during her trial. If she could have been tried *in absentia*, she might even then, have been forgiven, because the journal, after all these years of editing and re-writing came very close to being a masterpiece of hypocrisy.

There was, also, the mitigating passage of time in Mathilde's favour. By the year she finally went on trial, not only were many of the people she had betrayed, dead, but even those, like Pierre de Vomécourt, who would be summoned by the state as witnesses against her, were like millions of others who had survived the holocaust, trying to reestablish their lives in ways which had nothing to do with the war; they did not want to be dragged back through memory to those earlier times. Even the newspapers, which tried to make such a stirring episode of the more spectacular Nuremberg trials, for the most part, faced a jaded, apathetic audience. It was over, and it was done; the cost had been terrible. A surfeited world did not want to look back; it wanted to look forward. As Mathilde had written, not entirely with honesty, but with words fitting the moment, "everything was permitted to us without remorse and without regret". People, by the year Mathilde went on trial in 1949, were willing to concede something close to that. What was done, had been done, and most people were not heroes or heroines. Let sleeping dogs lie, let the past belong to the past. A thing which was done on Monday, became history on Tuesday; it could never be undone. There have never been any easy avenues through life; if a person lives out only part of their mature years, they will experience shame and sorrow and self-revulsion, and if they happen to be a woman, with every inherent frailty of all women, and are hurled into a cauldron of disorder and madness, what is to be expected of them that other people are entitled to sit in judgment upon?

The mood in France was like that, in 1949. The nation's most calamitous ordeal was over, and for every hero such as Pierre de Vomécourt, there were a thousand Mathilde Carrés or Renée Bornis.

But, for all her studied efforts at lyrical rhetoric, Mathilde could not entirely exclude revelations of her actual self. Commenting on her betrayals, she once said: "I only denounced the more stupid ones." And again, when queried on her reasons for betraying so many people to the Germans, her retort was: "There had to be victims. ... I had sometimes to sacrifice men ... that is just the fortune of war."

When it was clear that the time for her trial was drawing close, Mathilde's energy re-emerged. After those long years of regimented inactivity, she once again became as tireless and resourceful as she had been almost ten years earlier when she had helped Armand create Inter-Allied.

Her defence attorney was Maitre Albert Naud, not only a

lawyer of great ability, but a Frenchman who knew something
about betrayal and imprisonment, having been caught and
incarcerated by the Germans as the result of war-time
underground activities. He was to prove himself to be
precisely the man for the defence. At once, a favourable *rapport*
was established between Mathilde and this shrewd, capable
French barrister. He went into his assignment with calm and
deliberate objectivity. After several conferences with
Mathilde, Maitre Naud sent out to locate friendly witnesses.
It did not prove to be as difficult an undertaking as one might
have thought; for example, people who had served in the
Vichy *Deuxième Bureau* could testify that Mathilde had
co-operated with them, which she had, prior to going over to
the Germans. There were also others who had known
Mathilde prior to her defection, including another barrister,
Maitre Brault, who could testify that at one time she had
incurred risks by serving the Allies.

Of course, there were also people who could have testified
that Mathilde had, for about ten months after the fall of
France, been a loyal, energetic patriot, but who chose not to
testify so as a result of her subsequent treachery.

The British were contacted. It was hoped that they might
be willing to concede that Mathilde had, before and after her
defection, served them well. It was a vain hope. The British
were not only reticent, they were unwilling to become involved
in the defence of a woman they knew had almost nonchalantly
betrayed them, as well as her own most intimate friends and
associates.

Mathilde's reaction to the British position was
characteristic. She had, like Hugo Bleicher, come to the
conclusion long ago, that the British were a detestable people.
She had, she said, always kept faith with the British, had
served them with "hundred per cent" loyalty, and the least
they could do would be to send someone from their
Intelligence establishment to Paris to attend her trial.

Maitre Naud's efforts were also unavailing outside the areas
of British Intelligence. Mathilde had met a number of people
during her stay in England, who had not been of the secret
services. He sought their cooperation, too, without success.

Among the British the attitude seemed to be that Mathilde Carré was a French problem, not a British one, and it was difficult to fault that reasoning. If it had ever been otherwise, Mathilde could very well have been tried and put to death during her imprisonment in England. But Mathilde did not yield. She told Maitre Naud he should contact Ben Cowburn, among others. She even urged him to try and entice Colonel Buckmaster, the man she had wanted to kill, to come to Paris for the trial. She became almost shrewish in her demands, but she had no illusions; she was fighting for her life. Maitre Naud was always sympathetic, always willing to listen. Nor were all of Mathilde's arguments specious; she, too, had been educated in the law.

She wanted Hugo Bleicher at the trial, but since the war's end, Bleicher, who had for a time been a French captive, and whose position even as late as 1949 was not entirely secure, because of his association with the German Intelligence organizations, was unwilling to come to Paris. Nor could he be ordered to do so. His residence was within the British zone of occupation, at Hamburg, and whether it was entirely his own reluctance, or whether he may have been influenced by the British position towards Mathilde's forthcoming trial, the end result was the same. He refused to appear.

Maitre Naud's reaction to having Bleicher, the former *Abwehr* intriguist, face a French court, a French judge and jury, could have been excused if it lacked enthusiasm. His defence of Mathilde had to be founded, not upon her perfidy, of which Bleicher was a major part, but upon her female helplessness in the face of events over which she had had no control, and also upon the manner in which she had aided the Allies before and after her association with Bleicher.

As for Bleicher, who was by this time again established in business in Germany, and re-united with his family, it was the same story as it was for millions of other former participants in the war: he preferred not to be dragged back into it again. (Years later, though, Hugo Bleicher did evince a willingness to reminisce – for money, and for no other consideration.)

As the time of her trial drew closer, Mathilde's anxieties understandably increased. She sought constantly to have conferences with Maitre Naud, and once she wrote him: "For pity's sake, do not leave me in uncertainty or ignorance!"

For his part, Maitre Naud had worked up a creditable defence, in the light of what he had to work with, and in view of the grave charges against his client. He had his share of disappointments, too. When he sought access to the deposition Bleicher had given the French authorities, when he had been their prisoner, with the view of using this in Mathilde's defence, he had to accept a decision that this could not be introduced at the trial. An assumption in this regard could be made that the French government chose not to have this document made public on the grounds that Bleicher's statements, as a result of his *Abwehr* affiliation, could have revealed a lot more than was necessary, or even desirable, for the general public to know. It was a fact that French collaborationists had been vastly more numerous, and also more highly placed, than the world suspected. It would have helped no one, not even Mathilde, if this embarrassing information got out.

Another disappointment for Maitre Naud, was the stand taken by Armand – Roman Czerniawski – repatriated, finally, and in England. He declined to be present at Mathilde's trial, or to send along a statement, and again, as in the case of Hugo Bleicher, this may have been the result of personal reluctance, or it may have been the result of a suggestion originating with British Intelligence. Armand could have helped establish the fact that Mathilde's early efforts in the cause of the Allies had been valuable, but of all the people Mathilde had betrayed, none had as valid a reason to despise her now; Armand had personally witnessed the death of his friends at Mathausen, and had seen the irreversible deterioration of those who had not died there.

It was difficult for Mathilde's lawyer to secure really worthwhile defence witnesses. Those, like the members of Vichy's *Deuxième Bureau*, whom he could subpoena, and whose connections were clouded by either suspected pro-German sentiments, or a lack of a genuine attitude of resistance, could harm more than they could help. A French jury could not be expected to listen favourably to a witness whose wartime past was itself, suspect.

There was another possible witness, René Aubertin, who had known Mathilde long before her defection. Aubertin had known her as a child. He had been her friend and her confidant. He had gone through the bad days immediately after the French collapse with her. They had been, if not lovers, then certainly very close to it, over a considerable period of time. If anyone could have tried to explain this bizarre woman who could only really function if she had someone else's strength to draw upon, it would have been René Aubertin. But he had been recruited as a witness for the prosecution.

As the time for the trial came closer, Mathilde's efforts at defence increased. She and Maitre Naud had frequent meetings, and between these times, she sent him letters. On the other side, the Public Prosecutor, an equally astute barrister by the name of Becognée, had not been idle. He had been quietly and assiduously laying a solid foundation for the state. One of his principal witnesses was to be Paul de Vomécourt – Lucas. Others included Maitre Brault, Wladimir Lipsky, Henri Tabet, Renée Borni, and Mirielle Lejeune, whose husband had died at Mathausen. Of this coterie, Renée Borni was to be tried along with Mathilde, but for two reasons it was not to be expected that Renée would feel the full weight of French justice. The first reason was simply because no one at the trial, or before, ever considered Renée as anything more than a dim-witted, compliant, totally dominatable, individual. The second reason was because, when the trial began, she had to be carried into the room on a bed. She was suffering from a serious illness, and besides the strain which she visibly underwent during the days in court, which brought frequent bouts of quaking and tears, Renée, regardless of her sentence, was not going to survive for long.

Finally, on 3rd January 1949, the trial opened. Presiding as President of the Court of Justice was Judge Drappier. According to the official prelude, the court was to hear evidence in the matter of Mathilde Carré, sometimes known as the Cat, and Borni, Madame Renée, also known as 'Violette', widow of Lunéville.

The alleged crime in both cases was "Intelligence with the Enemy". Against Mathilde Carré the charges specified betrayal into the hands of the enemy of thirty five people, roughly one-third the actual number she betrayed. Against Renée the charge was one which had, by 1949, assumed an almost prosaic sameness – collaboration with the enemy; and even if Renée had not involuntarily aroused the pity of the courtroom, and the jury, she could have received no worse sentence than thousands like her had received, as a result of their fear, their bewilderment, and their inherent human weakness.

19

The Cat at Bay

According to the French code of legal procedure, a defendant is first examined by a magistrate, before the legal charges are entered, and if this may appear unique by the standards of British and American law, both founded upon Saxon law which requires an uninformed and impartial tribunal, it nevertheless is the French custom, and Mathilde's examination by a court magistrate revealed her basic defence tactic, which was to be, that, while she was aiding the Germans, she was doing so only in order to gain their confidence in order to betray them to the Allies, and also because she could not have done otherwise.

It did not appear to be much of a base to build a defence upon, since, the State would produce witnesses to swear she had not only willingly collaborated, but that she had voluntarily betrayed people it had not been necessary to betray at all. But there had to be a basis of some kind, certainly, and throwing oneself upon the mercy of the court in a case where conviction carried an obligatory sentence of death, was not to be considered. The death sentence was not mandatory; it was in fact, the maximum sentence, but it had been handed down often, in cases like Mathilde's, and it had been carried out as well. Therefore pleading extenuating circumstance, alone, without some foundation for justification, could be a very risky thing to do. Neither Maitre Naud or Mathilde were ever serious in their consideration of any course except the one they chose.

Mathilde's appearance in court was ambivalent, for while she appeared dressed very modestly in a neat dark skirt and white blouse, with a minimum of cosmetics, suggesting a demure, correctly repentant individual, she frequently made startling remarks, and annoyed almost everyone by an expression of hard-faced ruthlessness, and also by chewing gum, sneering, indicating disgust, contempt and scorn.

She wore her black hair in the neat manner which had been characteristic of her for so long, brushed until it shone, brushed in a straight line across the forehead, and reaching only two or three inches below the ears. She wore no earrings, no jewellery at all, and except for her glasses, often removed as she sat motionless in the dock staring impassively at a witness who was testifying, her face was entirely unrelieved by adornment. For the four days she was on trial, Mathilde's interest was intense. When she disagreed with what was said, her face reflected it. When she was angered, or contemptuous, these emotions also showed.

She remained, right up to the last, defiant and hostile. She did nothing by her manner to arouse sympathy nor compassion among the spectators. One news reporter wrote that she resembled a serpent more than a cat. Another reporter, a woman, who might have been expected to pity this small fellow-creature, wrote that Mathilde showed cynicism, insolence, and a clear and obvious hardness.

Madame Belard was of little help, either. She talked of her honourable family, of her brave son, who had been a St Cyr cadet, of her husband's sacrifices in two wars, of her courageous daughter whose invaluable asssistance to the Allies, and particularly to the British, was being repaid in this deplorable manner.

Maitre Naud had his work cut out for him. His client was not a repentent, grief-stricken girl; she was a woman one year away from being forty years of age, who was fiercely antagonistic to the court. Unlike Renée Borni, who lay wan and wasted on her bed, large, dark eyes mirroring mental as well as physical anguish, Mathilde never lost her poise, was a picture of robust health, and from time to time, fastened her green stare upon a witness with obvious baleful malevolence. By expression alone, she impressed people in the courtroom with her capacity for ruthlessness, with her unshakeable conviction that she alone mattered.

The initial presentation of facts took up Mathilde's life as it began with the fall of France, with her service as a nurse, for which she was presented a decoration and traced out her difficulties during those harrowing months, then moved ahead to her cooperation with the Pole, Roman Czerniawski, in seeking to organize the Inter-Allied underground network. Mathilde listened intently, rarely moving in her position behind the raised, dark wooden dock. As long as this droning recitation was under way, her features were wary but composed, but as the summary moved towards that sequence of events which began at dawn, the morning the Germans burst in upon Armand at the Villa Léandre, then apprehended Mathilde on the rue Cortet, the prisoner's concern became quietly intense. Ultimately, then, the recitation began to delve into her relationship with the enemy, and with a particular enemy, Hugo Bleicher.

Mathilde, leaning forward with her chin resting upon clasped hands atop the dock, paid particular attention to the allegations now being made – and got quite a surprise. M. Drappier, reading from a deposition Bleicher had given the court, evidently without Mathilde's knowledge, or the knowledge of Maitre Naud, said that although Bleicher had admitted to having known the defendant intimately upon a number of occasions, he confessed to having never achieved any physical satisfaction during those intimate moments.

That was too much. Mathilde was a Frenchwoman; a person whose intense sexuality was intermingled with her pride. She was not as stung by many later allegations charging her with treason, even malice, as she was by this charge that she had not been a satisfactory lover. She exclaimed loudly and very indignantly that this charge was only true when she had, not, upon occasion, "been nice" to Bleicher.

When she was asked under interrogation whether it had been necessary to become the mistress of Bleicher, her answer was to the effect that of course it had been. When she was asked if she could not have put this off; if it had been obligatory that she, the widow of a French officer, become "the mistress of a German sergeant", she demanded whether she must relate in detail how Bleicher had locked the bedroom door that first night at *Abwehr* St Germaine, and what had then ensued. M. Drappier replied that it was not necessary to go into detail, but was she not revolted at the prospect? Mathild said, "Yes, it did shock me . . .".

"And nevertheless," persisted M. Drappier, "you went to bed with him?"

Mathilde was exasperated, "Well," she retorted, "what else could I do?"

There were a number of other allusions to Mathilde's love life. One came about when Henri Tabet, the radioman who had first been an operator for Inter-Allied, and who subsequently worked for Bleicher, after Mathilde had helped the Germans track him down, was brought forth to give testimony.

It started innocently enough, with Tabet being asked the routine question of whether he knew the defendant, Mathilde Carré. Tabet's reply was: "Yes, I was on very intimate terms with her indeed".

This stung Mathilde to a swift and indignant retort. "That is not true. I never went to bed with members of the organization!"

Henri Tabet snapped back. "If you had a beauty-mark anywhere I would have been able to say where it was, but you do not have, and that is the truth!"

In other ways, too, Mathilde helped M. Becognée, the prosecutor, and one can imagine Maitre Naud's exasperation as his client was repeatedly baited into making the most injurious retorts. It was said that she had envisioned herself as a new and greater Mata Hari. She seemed to delight in hearing things like this being said about her, but she steadfastly adhered to her story of aiding the Germans solely so that she could ultimately betray them to the Allies. And just as consistently, the Public Prosecutor punched that aspect of the defence full of holes. For example, when a courier of Inter-Allied named Jean Dupré, was interrogated, he related how, upon being taken to Hotel Edouard VII for questioning, and seeing Mathilde there, he had assumed she too had been captured, so, when the Germans asked Dupré if he recognized her, he had denied ever having seen her before, believing that in this way he might protect her. Mathilde had turned on Dupré in anger. "What did you say? You never saw me before? Of course you have." She then told the Germans, "That is the man. You may carry on."

This did not sound like the statement of a woman seeking to help the Allies and hoodwink the Germans.

Again, when Mirielle Lejeune was being questioned, she told how Mathilde had said of Bleicher, who was with her that day, "Look, he is my new lover."

She did not help the defence, either, when she sneered at one of the men of the *Deuxième Bureau*, Colonel Achard, who testified that she had helped his agency; he called her an "admirable woman", but when it was pointed out that Mathilde had tried to lure him to Paris, ostensibly to deliver him to the *Abwehr*, she scoffed, saying she made no such effort, because, "the Colonel was not important enough to be of much interest to the Germans".

The other member of the *Deuxième Bureau*, whose name was Simonneau, (they were the two men who had taught Mathilde some of the tricks of the espionage trade during her visit to Vichy for Armand during Inter-Allied's early days) testified in private, on the grounds that it was not the policy of the French espionage establishment to appear, officially, in public, which was understandable except for one thing: most of the spectators knew who he was, and it was a certainty that the active participants knew.

One of the most noticeable principals was René Aubertin. He told a hushed courtroom how he had watched men die at Mathausen, how he and the others Mathilde had betrayed, had agreed that, should they survive they would appear as witnesses against Mathilde. "I promised my comrades at Mathausen," he related, "that ... I would testify truly but without hatred." He said that the simple truth was that Mathilde had "preferred her own life to that of thirty-five other people".

He named some of the Cat's victims: Lucien de Roquigny, who was "literally beaten to death". He recalled the Hugentoblers, especially Madame Hugentobler whose frantic worry for her baby had driven her to suicide; he remembered other incidents of callous brutality. The Cat sat stoically silent as did Maitre Naud when Aubertin quietly and dispassionately, but obviously under great emotional strain, did exactly what he had sworn at Mathausen he would; he testified truthfully and without hatred.

It was Maitre Brault who told the court in his opinion Mathilde's desire was to be a second Mata Hari "either a French or a German one, to her it really did not matter". He also told of introducing Mathilde to Pierre de Vomécourt, who was sitting quietly in the courtroom, and said that he would have done better to have broken his arm than to have trusted her. Maitre Brault made an excellent witness – for the prosecution.

Madame Belard was also called up. She faced the court in an attitude of indignation. The Belards, she said, were an honourable French family. No Belard would betray France. Throughout the war she and her husband had kept of picture of their brave son, the St Cyr Cadet, upon the wall of their flat, and also a French flag, whereupon the judge remarked that, nevertheless, Madame had served lunch to Bleicher, the *Abwehr* sergeant, within sight of that flag, and Madame came right back with a typical retort.

"Yes, but I insulted him for more than two hours."

Madame dramatized her statements, she dabbed at her eyes when this seemed to be called for. She gestured. She showed hauteur, as well as a slump of dejection, as though she were a poor, bewildered mother begging for sympathy for her daughter. And she succeeded rather well in alienating the courtroom. Even Mathilde was disgusted. She said to Maitre Naud, "she is making herself ridiculous". But to many of the spectators, Madame Belard was doing more; she was showing them that if Mathilde was a prevaricator and a hypocrite, she probably came by it naturally.

Still, this was evidently the only way Madame Belard knew how to fight for her daughter's life, and it was increasingly apparent as the trial went from its first to its second and third days, that Mathilde was losing ground very steadily. The death penalty was coming closer.

Madame even pleaded with René Aubertin. She said to him, that her daughter had only done what she did "to save you all and now only you can save her". Madame was out of touch with reality, for which she could possibly be excused, but regardless of that, her court appearance was another nail in her daughter's coffin.

The trial lasted from 3rd January to 7th January. It may have occurred to Mathilde, as it surely occurred to others, that this very interesting and very treacherous woman deserved more publicity than she was getting.

The courtroom did not lack spectators. There was news coverage. Mathilde Carré's case was certainly more intriguing than most trials of collaborationists. Every element was present to assure, normally, a wider public exposure, but the newspapers, excluding the limited-circulation editions published for former members of the underground organizations, hardly mentioned the trial, either during its course or afterwards.

For one thing, the spectacular Nuremberg trials of Germany's war criminals had come and gone by 1949. On 20th November 1946, the trial of major Nazi leaders opened at Nuremberg before an Allied Tribunal, which was the beginning of a very prolonged session of war-crime trials. Elsewhere, in all the Allied zones of Occupied Germany, as well as in the restored nations such as Poland, Holland, Norway, and France, there had been more trials. People did not forget, they were simply weary of war-crime trials.

Also, by 1949, the war years had been superseded by a very uneasy 'peace'. The Soviet Union had blockaded Berlin, and Allied aircraft had to fly in supplies. Friction between the Russians and their former war-time allies was approaching a point of distinct unpleasantness. A great many harbingers of an uncertain future, for France, as well as most other countries, made the trial of one Frenchwoman seem almost insignificant, and perhaps it was. But for a fact, the Carré-Borni trial received only terse and minimal coverage.

In many ways Mathilde herself was at fault. She failed to inspire sympathy or even pity. She showed contempt for the legal processes, indignation over statements of witnesses, and even scorn for those seeking in some way to help her.

Without prompting by M. Becognée of the prosecution, Mathilde seized the initiative, became the centre of attention as often as she could, and made statements that left no doubt but that she had served the Germans willingly and had not, as her defence claimed, been projected into a situation beyond her control.

Just once, during the long parade of witnesses, did she sit completely silent, and show nothing on her face. That was when Pierre de Vomécourt was called up.

He told, quietly, how he had met Mathilde, through Maitre Brault, and how he had considered killing her when he discovered that, as a double agent of the Germans, she had voluntarily betrayed as many members of the underground as she could, and considered it probable that she would also betray him, as well as Ben Cowburn, Roger Cottin, and others whom she knew had associated with de Vomécourt.

Mathilde's lawyer asked de Vomécourt if he believed Mathilde was sincere when she told him she wished to revert to her former status as an Allied agent, and thus make amends?

De Vomécourt replied that, yes, he thought Mathilde had been sincere, at that moment. But he also said that Mathilde had not told him the complete truth about her relationship with the Germans, nor the full extent of her perfidy, until he had become sufficiently sceptical of her to affect a confrontation. But in fairness and candour, he had to admit that once she had decided to cooperate with him, she had undergone considerable peril and hardship, and remained loyal to him right up to the moment they were eventually rescued by the MTB and taken to England.

The de Vomécourt statements brought forth no new testimony. Except for the prosecution's totally adverse presentation, most of the defence's case could have been rather well summarized by de Vomécourt: Mathilde had co-operated. The difficulty arose over the fact that she had co-operated as willingly, and as voluntarily with the Germans as she had with the Allies, and as a voluntary assistant of the *Abwehr*, she had been responsible for the anguish, and the death of a great number of people.

Finally, then, the case was presented to the jury. Maitre Naud made his presentation by reminding the jury that

Mathilde's lapse had not even been two months long, and that afterwards, she had willingly gone back to serve the Allies. He asked if she had done wrong in wanting to live? Furthermore, Mathilde, he said, had only been bait used by the unscrupulous *Abwehr* and Hugo Bleicher. He was not begging for acquittal, he was pleading for Mathilde's life.

Monsieur Becognée had the advantage. Cleverly, he quoted from Mathilde's journal, *Memoirs Of A Cat*. He read remarks she had written that showed cruelty, insensitivity, and cynicism. He called her a "brain without a heart" and said she was amoral – "a woman without scruples". He called on the jury to remember all those people she had "denounced . . . and the dead, and all of those who suffered through this woman's perfidy. . . . Think of those who today lie dead through her responsibility – and hers alone. . . . She betrayed her cause in a manner which I can find no words to pardon . . . with a heavy heart . . . I now ask you to punish this woman with the supreme penalty for traitors – with the penalty of death."

Throughout M. Becognée's oration, Mathilde had sat quite still, watching him – chewing gum, and faintly, contemptuously, smiling.

The other defendant, Renée Borni, was almost lost sight of. Nevertheless, she was also summarized before the jury, but no one really expected her to be severely sentenced – nor was she. When the jury handed in its decision, Renée Borni was found guilty of collaboration, of "Intelligence with the enemy", but with a recommendation for mercy on the grounds of "extenuating circumstances".

For Mathilde Carré, the jury had a different decision. She was sentenced to death, the maximum penalty for the crimes alleged against her. M. Drappier read the verdict to a silent chamber: Death, confiscation of all personal affects, national indignity, and she, or her estate, was to pay four-fifths of all expenses incurred by her trial. Mathilde stood impassively, leaning slightly upon the railing of the prisoner's dock, and when the sentence had been read, she again showed that faint expression of contempt.

20
The Cat's Finale

If Mathilde had expected leniency, or even a sentence based upon mitigation, she now knew that these things were not to be. Her future held a bleak prospect. She would be shot to death in the yard of a French prison.

Presumably, a person in Mathilde's position, after the sentencing, would feel a host of unpleasant emotions, and would perhaps be motivated in most of what they said and did by a degree of fatalism – there would no longer be much reason to prevaricate.

Mathilde wrote to her attorney that now, under sentence of death, she had no reason to conceal things, and on that basis, she asked him not to believe all the uncomplimentary things which had been said about her by the prosecution's witnesses. More revealingly, she also wrote to Maitre Naud that, for many years, lately, she had been unable to be with anyone from whom she could draw strength, but the exact words were: "I have not had anyone to whom I could show myself as I really am".

She was, she said, at the end of her strength. She had not been guilty, she wrote, of everything which had been alleged against her. Finally, she wished in the little time left her, to do good works among mankind, to spread as much happiness as she could, in the time left to her.

In closing one letter to Maitre Naud, she asked him to do everything he could to get her out of "this awful cell and this prison of Fresnes". She was housed in the same place where many of her victims had awaited their equally dolorous fate, with the difference being that for those others there had been no appeal, while for Mathilde there did exist at least a final hope, one which Maitre Naud did not neglect.

He appealed to the courts for mercy. Not clemency, but

recognition of the fact that Mathilde had, at one time, risked her life for the cause which had finally triumphed, and this, at least, certainly lifted her from the category of unpardonable collaborationist.

He further mentioned in his appeal, that at the time of Armand's arrest by the Germans, there had been the most revealing documents in the Villa Léandre apartment; that the *Abwehr* would have been able, through this cavalier carelessness, to apprehend the Inter-Allied membership, even if Mathilde had not cooperated with her captors.

Maitre Brault had openly said that Armand's recklessness in this regard had frightened him, even in the early days of the Inter-Allied-British connection.

As for Mathilde's liaison with Hugo Bleicher, according to Maitre Naud's reasoning, that was not what she had been on trial about. As for the German association, Maitre Naud conceded her mistake in this respect, but she had risked her life before and after this unfortunate interlude, and she had been of value to the Allied cause.

He sought understanding as much as mitigation, and it was entirely possible to hope his efforts might be successful, since the plea was directed to men in high office who had not attended the trial, did not know Mathilde Carré, and who were, like everyone, weary of the war. In May of 1949, Maitre Naud was notified that his client's case had been reviewed. The determination was that the sentence of death should be commuted to life imprisonment.

For Mathilde, the commutation had to be a mixed blessing. After seven years of imprisonment, death of course was neither preferable nor desirable, but the prospect of spending the duration of her mortal existence behind stone walls, was only a little better.

She changed, of course. She had not been the chic, voluptuous, green-eyed, passionate lover of men since her incarceration in England. Her health deteriorated somewhat, but most noticeable was her failing eyesight.

She drew into herself more and more, as the years passed, but excepting a few people who remembered, those she had harmed or their families, the public in France had very little interest in Mathilde Carré.

Later, when her sentence was reduced, there was very little actual opposition, although the fraternal organizations of former underground members were quick to protest against all acts of clemency for collaborationists, and protested against such an act favouring Mathilde.

Finally, twelve years after her apprehension by the British in 1954, Mathilde Carré was granted a pardon. When she came back to the world of choices, so many things had changed it was like visiting a new land. The drab, dreary Paris of the war-years was just a memory. She encountered comfortable adults who had reached maturity, plump, sleek, secure, without realizing what the Occupation had really been like. They had been children back during those bad years.

Twelve years made a great difference. Mathilde's eye trouble was becoming increasingly unresponsive to treatment. She wore glasses constantly now, usually with dark-tinted lenses. She lived for a time with her parents on the Avenue des Gobelins, where large, domineering Madame Belard looked after her, still complaining bitterly that the British could have done more for her daughter, who had served them so unstintingly, but eventually Mathilde left the Belard domicile. There was some reference to her life being in danger, possibly from former underground associates, or the survivors of those Mathilde had betrayed to the Germans. It was possible, of course, but after all those years, not very probable. In any event, Mathilde Carré unofficially died that year, 1954. She moved to a small town in the countryside, assumed another name, and was not seen again by anyone but her family, all of whom absolutely refused to divulge her whereabouts.

Mathilde was alive in 1960. At least there were allegations to that effect. She could still be alive in 1975; she would now be sixty-five years of age, but whether she is or not, she would no longer be recognizable as the Cat of the Second World War and of espionage fame – or notoriety.

Bibliography

An Encyclopaedia of World History, ed. William L. Langer, Harrap, 1969

Inside S.O.E., E.H. Cookridge, Arthur Barker, 1966

France Reborn, Jean Améry, Charles Scribner's Sons

Seven Times Seven Days, Emmanuel d'Astier De La Vigerie, MacGibbon & Kee Co., 1958

They Fought Alone, Maurice Buckmaster, Odhams, 1958

A World In Flames, Martha Byrd Hoyle, Atheneum Books Inc., 1970

Gestapo, Edward Crankshaw, Putnam & Co. Ltd, 1956

Profile Of The Nations, (atlas), Hammond Inc.

The Cat With Two Faces, Gordon Young, Putnam & Co. Ltd, 1957

The Second World War, Vols 1 and 2, Winston Churchill, Cassell, 1948-9

The Theory And Practice Of Hell, Eugen Kogon, Secker & Warburg, 1950

The German General Staff, Walter Görlitz, Hollis & Carter Ltd, 1953

The Scourge Of The Swastika, Lord Russell Of Liverpool, Cassell 1954

Crusade In Europe, Dwight D. Eisenhower, Heinemann, 1949

No Bugles For Spies, Robert Hayden Alcorn, Jarrolds, 1963

Mein Kampf, Adolf Hitler, Hurst & Blackett Ltd, 1938

Duel Of Wits, Peter Churchill, Transworld Publications, 1955

History Of The Second World War, ed. Basil Liddell Hart, Cassell, 1970

Specially Employed, Maurice Buckmaster, Batchworth Ltd, 1952

No Cloak, No Dagger, Ben Cowburn, Jarrolds, 1960

S.O.E. In France, M.R.D. Foote, H.M.S.O.

Craft Of Intelligence, Allen Dulles, Weidenfeld & Nicholson, 1964

Confessions Of A Special Agent, Jack Evans, Robert Hale, 1957

German Military Intelligence, P. Leverkuehn, Weidenfeld & Nicholson, 1954

An Army Of Amateurs, Philippe de Vomécourt, Doubleday & Co., 1961

Index